Empath

Harnessing the Power of Empathic Abilities

(Channel Your Inner Abilities and Unlock Your Hidden Potentia)

Antonio Bailey

I0089823

Published By **Bella Frost**

Antonio Bailey

Empath: Harnessing the Power of Empathic Abilities (Channel Your Inner Abilities and Unlock Your Hidden Potentia)

ISBN   978-1-7779883-9-5

No part of this guidebook shall be reproduced in any form without permission in writing from the publisher except in the case of brief quotations embodied in critical articles or reviews.

Legal & Disclaimer

The information contained in this book is not designed to replace or take the place of any form of medicine or professional medical advice. The information in this book has been provided for educational & entertainment purposes only.

The information contained in this book has been compiled from sources deemed reliable, and it is accurate to the best of the Author's knowledge; however, the Author cannot guarantee its accuracy and validity and cannot be held liable for any errors or omissions. Changes are periodically made to this book. You must consult your doctor or get professional medical advice before using any of the suggested remedies, techniques, or information in this book.

Table Of Contents

Chapter 1: Understanding Empathy

(What is empathy and the way does it paintings?, Different styles of empathy, How empathy affects the thoughts, frame, and emotions)

Understanding empathy & How does it art work?

Empathy is the potential to experience and recognize the emotions, feelings, and reports of others. It consists of putting ourselves in a person else's footwear, and experiencing the sector from their thoughts-set.

Empathy can paintings in splendid methods, relying at the kind of empathy involved. There are numerous styles of empathy, together with:

Cognitive empathy: This includes understanding the thoughts and feelings of others, without necessarily sharing their feelings. It lets in us to be greater attuned to the desires and perspectives of others.

Emotional empathy: This involves definitely sharing in the emotions of others. When we experience emotional empathy, we revel in the identical feelings as the person we are empathizing with.

Compassionate empathy: This includes the usage of empathy to inspire us to accomplish that to help others. It allows us to feel the ache of others and be moved to help alleviate their struggling.

Empathy is a complex phenomenon that includes many one-of-a-type components of the thoughts, which consist of the prefrontal cortex, the insula, and the reflect neuron tool. When we empathize with others, our brains activate some of the equal regions which can be concerned in experiencing those emotions ourselves. This can reason emotions of connection and records, further to a deeper appreciation for the critiques of others.

Different styles of Empathy:

proper here are numerous excellent kinds of empathy, which encompass:

Cognitive empathy: This is likewise referred to as mindset-taking, and includes knowledge the mind, emotions, and perspectives of others. It allows us to understand what others are going thru and reply because it need to be. Cognitive empathy is regularly associated with trouble-fixing, crucial wondering, and effective communique.

Emotional empathy: This is likewise known as affective empathy, and includes genuinely feeling the emotions of others. When we enjoy emotional empathy, we are able to percentage within the emotions of those round us, and recognize their emotional united states of america on a deeper degree. Emotional empathy can help us connect to others and display compassion and understanding.

Compassionate empathy: This is a aggregate of cognitive and emotional empathy, and consists of no longer best expertise the emotions of others, but also being stimulated to do so to assist them. When we revel in compassionate empathy, we are moved to alleviate the struggling of others and take steps to make their lives higher.

Somatic empathy: This consists of feeling bodily sensations in reaction to the stories of others. For instance, if a person describes feeling ache or discomfort, we may additionally enjoy a twinge in our personal body in reaction. Somatic empathy can assist us recognize the bodily studies of others and reply as it should be.

Spiritual empathy: This involves spotting and connecting with the spiritual or metaphysical factors of others. It permits us to understand the ideals and values of others on a deeper degree, and might help us discover commonplace floor and construct relationships based totally on shared values.

Overall, empathy is a complicated and multifaceted phenomenon which can occur in masses of taken into consideration certainly one of a type techniques. By statistics the distinctive sorts of empathy, we can come to be greater attuned to our personal empathic competencies and use them to connect with others and make a awesome distinction in the worldwide.

How empathy impacts the thoughts, frame, and feelings

Empathy may also moreover have profound effects on the thoughts, frame, and feelings. Here are a few examples of the manner empathy can effect one-of-a-type factors of our being:

Mind: Empathy can help us emerge as higher trouble-solvers, important thinkers, and communicators. When we're able to recognize the perspectives of others, we're able to make extra knowledgeable alternatives and navigate complex social conditions more efficaciously. Empathy also can assist us be more open-minded and accepting of diverse thoughts and viewpoints.

Body: Empathy might also have both exquisite and terrible outcomes at the frame. On one hand, feeling empathy can launch endorphins and specific experience-great chemical materials inside the mind, leading to a sense of pride and praise. On the opportunity hand, feeling too much empathy or being uncovered to the struggling of others can bring about strain, tension, or even physical symptoms and symptoms like headaches and muscle tension.

Chapter 2: The Challenges Of Being An Empath

(Common demanding situations confronted by means of using way of empaths, Dealing with weigh down and sensory overload, Coping with different human beings's feelings)

Common disturbing conditions confronted via the usage of manner of empaths

Empaths can face numerous challenges of their every day lives, which includes:

Emotional overload: Empaths can end up overwhelmed with the useful resource of the emotions of others, in particular if they may be significantly sensitive. They may additionally moreover feel tired, exhausted, or perhaps physical unwell after being in crowded or emotionally charged environments.

Difficulty placing boundaries: Empaths can also additionally have hassle putting obstacles and announcing no to others, specifically within the occasion that they revel in accountable or obligated to assist. This can result in emotions of resentment, burnout, and emotional exhaustion.

Absorbing bad strength: Empaths are especially attuned to the emotions of others, which means that they'll pick out up on terrible power and emotions extra with out hassle. This can reason emotions of anxiety, despair, or perhaps bodily signs like headaches and stomachaches.

Feeling isolated or misunderstood: Empaths can also revel in remoted or misunderstood through the use of others who do not percent their sensitivities or functionality to enjoy deeply. This can result in emotions of loneliness or a sense of no longer belonging.

Difficulty processing their non-public feelings: Empaths might also additionally emerge as so focused on the feelings of others that they forget their personal emotional dreams. They may also conflict to way and specific their non-public feelings, main to emotional bottling and a sense of inner turmoil.

It's essential for empaths to apprehend the ones traumatic situations and take steps to control them. This may encompass placing boundaries, practising self-care, and finding supportive businesses of like-minded individuals. By understanding and addressing those challenges, empaths can stay greater desirable and balanced lives, at the same time as however harnessing their particular devices of empathy and compassion.

Dealing with overwhelm and sensory overload:

Empaths can revel in sensory overload while they may be uncovered to overwhelming stimuli in conjunction with loud noises, crowds, or excessive feelings. This can bring about feelings of exhaustion, tension, and pressure. Here are some tips for dealing with weigh down and sensory overload:

Take breaks: If you are feeling beaten, take a wreck from the state of affairs and deliver yourself a while to recharge. This may contain stepping outdoor for some clean air, taking a brief walk, or locating a quiet space to meditate or lighten up.

Practice mindfulness: Mindfulness techniques such as deep respiratory, visualization, and body scans allow you to stay present in the 2d and manage overwhelming feelings.

Use grounding strategies: Grounding techniques at the side of the use of your senses to connect with your environment (e.G. Feeling the feel of a ground, noticing the colours round you, or listening to the sounds for your surroundings) will will let you enjoy greater centered and less crushed.

Set barriers: Setting boundaries is an vital part of managing sensory overload. This can also include saying "no" to sure requests, limiting your publicity to draining human beings or conditions, or taking breaks whilst you want them.

Practice self-care: Practicing self-care is critical for empaths, especially while dealing with weigh down and sensory overload. This can also contain engaging in sports activities sports that convey you delight, collectively with exercise, analyzing, or spending time with loved ones.

Seek assist: It may be beneficial to are looking for help from friends, family, or a therapist who's conscious your sensitivity and can offer steering and help.

Coping with different human beings's emotions:

As an empath, managing one-of-a-kind human beings's emotions can be a assignment. Here are some hints for handling different human beings's feelings:

Practice self-consciousness: It's important to be privy to your non-public emotions and barriers at the identical time as interacting with others. Take time to check in with your self and apprehend at the identical time as you experience beaten or worn-out.

Listen actively: Active listening includes giving your complete interest to the alternative individual and seeking to recognize their attitude. This will let you assemble rapport and enjoy extra related with the opportunity character.

Validate their feelings: Validation consists of acknowledging and accepting the opportunity individual's feelings, even in case you do no longer commonly consider them. This can help the other man or woman enjoy heard and understood.

Chapter 3: The Empath's Survival Kit

(Developing self-attention and self-care practices, Setting healthy obstacles, Clearing and defensive your energy, Learning to control and adjust your emotions)

The Empath's Survival Kit:

Self-attention

Developing self-focus and self-care practices is critical for empaths. This might also additionally contain training mindfulness, meditation, and unique relaxation techniques.

Developing self-interest and self-care practices is critical for empaths to maintain their properly-being and control their sensitivity. Here are some tips for growing self-consciousness and self-care practices:

Reflect on your feelings: Take time to reflect in your personal feelings and understand styles in your emotions and behaviors. This will let you higher understand your private dreams and triggers.

Practice mindfulness: Mindfulness techniques together with deep respiratory, meditation, and body scans will let you stay gift in the 2nd and manage overwhelming emotions.

Set obstacles: Setting limitations is an vital part of self-care. This may additionally moreover moreover contain pronouncing "no" to incredible requests, limiting your publicity to draining people or conditions, or taking breaks while you need them.

Engage in sports activities that deliver you pride: Engaging in sports activities that supply you pleasure and achievement will allow you to recharge and enjoy greater centered. This ought to probably contain pastimes, spending time with loved ones, or wearing out modern pursuits.

Take care of your bodily fitness: Taking care of your physical health via regular exercising, healthful eating, and ok sleep allow you to manipulate strain and hold your properly-being.

Seek guide: It can be beneficial to are trying to find help from friends, own family, or a therapist who is acquainted along with your sensitivity and can offer steerage and assist.

By developing self-awareness and self-care practices, empaths can higher manipulate their sensitivity and keep their well-being.

Setting Healthy Boundaries

Setting healthy barriers is likewise critical for protective an empath's energy and stopping burnout. This may additionally encompass saying "no" to pleasant requests or restricting the quantity of time spent with draining human beings. Setting healthy boundaries is an important part of self-deal with empaths. Here are a few suggestions for putting healthy barriers:

Identify your values and desires: Take time to understand your values and goals. This will let you decide what's essential to you and what boundaries you want to set to protect your nicely-being.

Communicate your barriers: Be smooth and direct even as talking your barriers to others. This can also additionally involve saying "no" to first rate requests or setting limits on how heaps time and strength you can commit to positive humans or conditions.

Learn to mention "no": Saying "no" may be hard for empaths, but it is an important part of setting obstacles. Practice saying "no" in a clean and direct manner that is respectful of the opportunity man or woman's emotions.

Respect others' barriers: Just as it's miles vital to set your non-public limitations, it's far vital to realize the boundaries of others. This can assist assemble be given as authentic with and appreciate for your relationships.

Take time for your self: Make time for self-care and prioritize sports activities that help you recharge and sense more centered. This may additionally moreover include placing apart time for pursuits, workout, or spending time with loved ones.

Seek help: It may be beneficial to are looking for for guide from friends, family, or a therapist who can offer guidance and assist as you navigate putting healthful barriers.

By setting healthful limitations, empaths can better guard their nicely-being and keep healthy relationships with others.

Clearing & Protecting

Clearing and shielding your energy can contain practices which consist of visualization, smudging, and energy recuperation.

As an empath, it's far vital to easy and protect your energy to save you your self from feeling beaten or tired. Here are a few pointers for clearing and protective your power:

Practice grounding strategies: Grounding techniques, which includes walking barefoot in nature or visualizing roots developing out of your ft into the earth, permit you to experience greater focused and linked to the prevailing second.

Use crystals and special tools: Crystals, which incorporates black tourmaline or amethyst, are believed to have protecting homes that might help clean and defend your power. You also can use tools like sage or palo santo to easy your area of terrible energy.

Practice visualization: Visualization strategies, which include imagining a defend of white mild spherical you or visualizing horrific power leaving your body, allow you to clear and shield your power.

Take breaks at the same time as wanted: Taking breaks even as you experience beaten or worn-out will assist you to recharge and reset your strength.

Set limitations: Setting limitations will can help you shield your energy from draining human beings or conditions. This may additionally comprise proscribing your exposure to high quality human beings or conditions or pronouncing "no" to wonderful requests.

Practice self-care: Practicing self-care is critical for empaths, especially close to clearing and protecting their strength. This can also additionally incorporate challenge sports that deliver you pride, which includes workout, meditation, or spending time in nature.

By clearing and protective your electricity, you could better control your sensitivity and maintain your well-being.

Learning to control and alter your emotions.

Learning to manipulate and adjust your own emotions is vital for empaths to keep away from being crushed by using the emotions of others. Learning to govern and adjust your feelings is crucial for empaths, who regularly experience deeply and can be greater prone to experiencing immoderate feelings. Here are a few suggestions for handling and regulating your feelings:

Identify your emotions: Take time to turn out to be aware about and label your feelings.

This will will let you better apprehend your feelings and take steps to manipulate them.

Here are some steps you could take that will help you pick out out your emotions as an empath:

1.   Pay hobby to bodily sensations: When you're experiencing emotions, you can feel physical sensations inclusive of anxiety for your chest, a knot to your stomach, or a lump to your throat. Take phrase of those physical sensations, and try to perceive which emotion they will be associated with.

2.   Take time for self-pondered photograph: Spend some time on my own every day to mirror to your feelings. You can also moreover locate it beneficial to hold a mag or write down your thoughts and feelings.

3.   Identify triggers: Pay interest to the conditions and people that reason strong emotional responses in you. Once you pick out your triggers, you may paintings to

manipulate your feelings on the same time as you come across them.

Practice mindfulness: Mindfulness techniques, which encompass deep respiratory or meditation, permit you to stay present inside the moment and control overwhelming feelings.

Here are some mindfulness techniques you could strive:

1. Mindful respiratory: Take a few moments to recognition to your breath. Pay interest to the feeling of the air moving inside and outside of your body. You can try counting your breaths or announcing a mantra to help you awareness.

2. Body take a look at: Lie down or sit down down in a cushty function and produce your interest to 1-of-a-type factors of your body, starting collectively along with your toes and walking your way as a good deal because the pinnacle of your head. Notice any sensations or emotions in each part of your frame.

three.   Mindful assertion: Choose an item, which includes a flower, a tree, or a piece of art work, and have a look at it cautiously. Notice the colours, textures, and shapes. Try to be honestly present within the second and attention at the data.

4.   Mindful strolling: Take a stroll outside and recognition on the sensations of your frame as you walk. Pay interest to the feeling of your feet touching the floor, the movement of your legs, and the rhythm of your breath.

five.   Mindful ingesting: Take a couple of minutes to consume a snack or a meal in silence. Focus at the taste, texture, and fragrance of the meals. Chew slowly and have amusing with each chew.

Develop coping strategies: Develop coping techniques that offer you with the outcomes you need, at the side of journaling, workout, or speaking to a depended on pal or therapist.

Here are some coping strategies for empaths:

1.   Set boundaries: Empaths will be predisposed to take within the feelings of those round them, so it's crucial to set barriers to defend your very very own emotional well-being. You can say no to humans whilst you need to, restrict your exposure to horrible facts or humans, or take breaks at the same time as you are feeling crushed.

2.   Practice self-care: Taking care of yourself is important for empaths. Make time for sports activities sports that deliver you satisfaction, at the side of reading a ebook, taking a bath, or going for a walk. Practice wholesome behavior, together with getting enough sleep, consuming nutritious factors, and exercise frequently.

three.   Develop a self-soothing recurring: When you are feeling beaten, it may be useful to have a self-soothing everyday to reveal to. This could probable embody deep breathing, meditation, yoga, or one-of-a-kind relaxation

23

strategies that help you experience calm and focused.

4. Connect with others: Empaths regularly advantage from connecting with exclusive like-minded human beings. Joining a useful resource enterprise, taking a category or workshop, or locating a network on-line will can help you experience understood and supported.

Practice self-compassion: Be type and compassionate with your self, especially whilst you are experiencing excessive feelings. Practice self-care and take time to do matters that make you experience proper.

Here are a few pointers for schooling self-compassion:

1. Practice mindfulness: Mindfulness will assist you to emerge as more aware of your thoughts and emotions with out judging them. This can be useful in growing self-compassion because it lets in you to famend

your feelings with out getting caught up in self-grievance or terrible self-speak.

2.   Treat yourself as you will treat a chum: Imagine what you can say to a pal who is going thru a difficult time. Try to provide your self the identical kindness and information which you may offer to someone you care approximately.

3.   Practice self-care: Taking care of your self physical, emotionally, and mentally is an essential part of self-compassion. This would probable embody getting sufficient sleep, ingesting nicely, exercising, spending time with buddies, or carrying out sports activities activities you revel in.

four.   Challenge horrible self-talk: Pay hobby to the awful self-talk that may be protecting you once more from training self-compassion. When you note awful mind, try to undertaking them via asking your self if they'll be clearly real.

5.   Forgive yourself: We all make errors, and it is important to forgive yourself at the same time as you do. Recognize that making errors is a everyday part of being human, and try to look at from your errors in place of beating your self up over them.

Learn to apprehend and manipulate triggers: Identify triggers that may result in overwhelming feelings, along facet incredible humans or situations, and have a observe techniques to control them.

Chapter 4: Empowering Your Empathy

(Developing instinct and psychic abilities, Using empathy as a device for recovery and connection, Building wholesome relationships as an empath)

Empowering Your Empathy

Developing your intuition

Developing intuition and psychic skills can help empaths higher apprehend and connect to others. Developing instinct and psychic skills can be a natural extension of being an empath. Here are some tips for growing these abilities:

Practice meditation: Meditation will can help you quiet your mind and track into your intuition. Start with only a few minutes of every day exercising and frequently growth the time as you turn out to be greater comfortable.

Listen in your intestine: Pay interest to your instincts and instinct. Trust your gut emotions, even supposing they do no longer make logical revel in.

Develop your psychic senses: There are four most important psychic senses: clairvoyance (clean seeing), clairaudience (clean listening to), clairsentience (smooth feeling), and claircognizance (clean know-how). Focus on developing the experience(s) that come maximum clearly to you.

Work with divination equipment: Tarot playing gambling playing cards, oracle gambling playing cards, and exclusive divination tools can be used to faucet into your instinct and psychic competencies.

Practice electricity paintings: Reiki, acupuncture, and particular sorts of energy art work will let you enlarge your sensitivity to power and track into your instinct.

Trust the approach: Developing your instinct and psychic talents takes time and exercising. Be affected character with yourself and acquire as real with the method.

By growing your instinct and psychic skills, you can benefit a deeper information of your self and others, and probable use those abilities to help others in a recuperation or recuperation functionality.

Using empathy as a device for healing and connection

Using empathy as a device for healing and connection can incorporate practices which incorporates active listening, validation, and compassion. Empathy may be a effective tool for recuperation and connection. Here are some processes that empaths can use their sensitivity to help others:

Active listening: Empaths are regularly expert listeners who can track into others' emotions and desires. By actively listening and empathizing with others, you can help them revel in heard and showed.

Compassionate communication: Empaths can use their sensitivity to talk with others in a compassionate and knowledge way. This can help collect deeper connections and acquire as genuine with.

Healing touch: If you are educated in a restoration modality like Reiki or massage treatment, you may use your sensitivity to strength and speak to to provide healing and relaxation to others.

Art remedy: Art treatment can be a effective way to connect with others and specific feelings. Empaths can use their sensitivity to create a steady and supportive area for others to discover their feelings thru artwork.

Storytelling: Empaths can use their sensitivity to hook up with others via the energy of storytelling. By sharing reminiscences of their non-public stories and struggles, they may help others experience much less by myself and further understood.

Support organizations: Empaths can use their sensitivity to create supportive groups and agencies wherein humans can join and proportion their opinions.

By using empathy as a tool for recovery and connection, empaths can create notable trade within the global and help others to heal and grow.

Building healthful relationships as an empath

Building healthy relationships as an empath can include locating those who admire and help your sensitivity, and placing clear verbal exchange and boundary expectations. Building wholesome relationships can be difficult for empaths who regularly sense deeply and can be more touchy to the feelings and energy of others. Here are a few tips for building healthful relationships as an empath:

Be selective with who you spend time with: It's essential for empaths to be selective with who they spend time with. Surround your self with folks who uplift and manual you, and avoid people who drain your strength.

Communicate your desires: Communicate your desires honestly to others, and set limitations to shield your strength. Let people realize at the same time as you want place or time by myself to recharge.

Practice self-care: Take care of your self and prioritize self-care. When you address yourself, you're higher prepared to reveal up in your relationships in a healthful and immoderate terrific way.

Listen on your instinct: Trust your instincts and pay hobby to your intuition almost about your relationships. If something does not enjoy proper, honor that feeling and take steps to address it.

Foster empathy on your relationships: Use your sensitivity to connect with others and understand their goals and emotions. Practice active listening and communicate in a compassionate and facts manner.

Chapter 5: Putting All Of It Collectively

(Creating a customised empathy survival plan, Overcoming commonplace roadblocks to empathy survival, Taking your empathy to the following degree)

Putting all of it Together

Creating a customized empathy survival plan

Creating a custom designed empathy survival plan includes incorporating strategies from all the preceding modules to create a tailor-made method that works awesome for each person. Creating a customized empathy survival plan can be a beneficial tool for empaths to manipulate their sensitivity and thrive in their day by day lives. Here are a few steps to developing an empathy survival plan:

Identify your triggers: Make a listing of situations or human beings that purpose your sensitivity. This can include crowds, conflict, poor human beings, or loud noises.

Develop coping strategies: Brainstorm coping strategies that be simply proper for you at the equal time as you feel crushed or overstimulated. This can include deep respiratory, meditation, taking a harm, or wearing out a chilled interest.

Set obstacles: Identify barriers as a manner to protect your energy and help you keep stability in your life. This can include placing limits on social engagements, announcing no to requests that do not align collectively collectively along with your values, or limiting your exposure to terrible people or situations.

Practice self-care: Develop a self-care normal that enables your physical, intellectual, and emotional properly-being. This can embody everyday workout, healthy ingesting, spending time in nature, or carrying out innovative sports.

Connect with others: Identify supportive friends, family members, or agencies that you can connect with and percentage your reviews with. Building a supportive community permit you to feel a whole lot less isolated and provide a source of consolation and know-how.

Review and modify your plan: Regularly overview your empathy survival plan and make changes as wanted. As you learn extra approximately your sensitivity and what works for you, your plan also can need to be up to date to mirror the ones modifications.

By developing a customized empathy survival plan, empaths can manipulate their sensitivity and thrive in their every day lives.

Overcoming not unusual roadblocks to empathy

Overcoming commonplace roadblocks to empathy survival also can moreover include addressing restricting ideals and awful self-speak, and developing a assist system.

While empathy may be a powerful tool for connection and information, there also are a few not unusual roadblocks which could intrude with our capacity to exercise empathy. Here are some techniques for overcoming those roadblocks:

Judgment: One of the most important roadblocks to empathy is judgment. When we pick out others, we are less likely so you can positioned ourselves of their shoes and understand their attitude. To overcome this roadblock, attempt to approach conditions with an open mind and withhold judgment till you have got were given more records.

Bias: Our biases also can get within the manner of empathy. We may also moreover have unconscious biases primarily based mostly on race, gender, or different factors that make it difficult to sincerely understand others. To triumph over this roadblock, it is critical to be aware of our biases and paintings to undertaking them.

Emotional overwhelm: When we are feeling overwhelmed thru the use of our very personal emotions, it could be difficult to song in to others' emotions and exercise empathy. To overcome this roadblock, exercise self-care and amplify coping techniques to manipulate your very personal emotions in order that you may be more present for others.

Lack of mindset: Sometimes we also can conflict to workout empathy because of the truth we in reality lack the perspective or enjoy to virtually apprehend what others are going via. To triumph over this roadblock, are looking for out possibilities to study more approximately specific views and tales.

Fear of vulnerability: Empathy requires a degree of vulnerability, as we need to be willing to connect to others on an emotional degree. To triumph over this roadblock, workout commencing up and sharing your very very personal reviews with relied on friends or circle of relatives individuals.

By spotting those roadblocks and strolling to overcome them, we can end up greater professional at working towards empathy and constructing stronger, more meaningful connections with others.

Taking your empathy to the subsequent diploma

Taking your empathy to the following level may additionally moreover include persevering with to enlarge your skills and abilities, and the usage of your sensitivity for exceptional alternate inside the global.

Taking your empathy to the subsequent diploma consists of growing your empathic abilities and the use of them to create outstanding alternate in the international. Here are a few strategies for taking your empathy to the subsequent diploma:

Practice active listening: Active listening involves no longer best being attentive to what others are announcing, but moreover paying attention to their nonverbal cues and emotions. By schooling energetic listening, you can deepen your information of others and assemble stronger connections.

Engage in attitude-taking: Perspective-taking entails placing yourself in a person else's shoes and seeing the vicinity from their trouble of view. By task attitude-taking, you could boom greater empathy and knowledge of others.

Develop your instinct: Intuition is a effective device for empaths, because it permits us to tune into our very very own feelings and the feelings of others. To expand your intuition, exercise mindfulness, meditation, and top notch strategies that help you come to be extra privy to your own feelings and the feelings of others.

Use your empathy to create extremely good alternate: Empathy may be a powerful device for growing first-class trade within the global. Use your empathy to propose for causes you care about, volunteer a while to assist others, or truely display kindness and compassion to those round you.

Seek out opportunities to take a look at and grow: Finally, preserve to are searching for for out possibilities to have a look at and boom as an empath. Read books and articles on empathy, attend workshops or trainings, and connect with other empaths to share research and techniques.

By taking those steps to increase your empathy and use it to create incredible alternate within the global, you can take your empathy to the subsequent level and make a actual difference in the lives of others.

Chapter 6: Know The Basics Of Empaths

Have you ever been accused of being overly sensitive or attuned? Do best individuals make you enjoy worn out after being with them for some time? Can you come across even as a person is not being completely honest with you? Do crowded locations make you anxious? Do you experience those emotions at the equal time as your buddy is reasonably happy or distressed? If you may affirmatively respond to those questions, you may be an empath—a totally precise elegance of human beings. Empaths possess a neurological mechanism that reacts proper away. The filters that exclusive people have to block off stimuli aren't there in us. As a give up quit result, the uplifting and distressing power within the worldwide around us is absorbed into our our our bodies.

It's like grasping something in hand with fifty arms instead of five because of the truth we are touchy. Excellent listeners, we are. According to investigate, 25 percentage of the populace is suffering from high sensitivity; but, sensitivity levels may additionally variety.

Empaths have frequently received advice to "increase a quite thick pores and skin" and be a great deal less "more sensitive." We aren't encouraged for our sensitivities as children or adults; we're chastised for them. Chronic tiredness and a preference to withdraw from the world could probably stop result from how annoying existence can on occasion sense. However, you will no longer trade your empathic skills for a few aspect at this stage. It lets in you to perceive the mysteries of the cosmos and experience pride past your most expectations.

Your capability to empathize hasn't continuously seemed as fantastic to you, even though. The frame of an empath is particular from that of various people. We revel in everything. Due to the porous nature of our our bodies, we're prone to soaking up each proper and terrible energies into our tissues, organs, and muscle mass. It has numerous large fitness implications. On the plus aspect, we are capable of enjoy the lifestyles, pride, and love of others internal ourselves. It is a exquisite treatment and feels top notch! Although, we also are able to sensing the anxiety, discomfort, and unpleasant emotions (especially even as they will be unsaid) of various human beings. As empaths, we also can emerge as exhausted and sick on the identical time as exposed to toxic human beings, loud noises, violent activity, hurrying, and screaming.

1.1 Outline of Empaths

Empathy is a sense or manner of being that allows one to narrate to every other character on a intellectual and emotional degree.

It particularly approach having the ability to "area oneself in a few different person's shoes" to extra simply recognise their sentiments or events. Whether personal or enterprise partnerships, it may useful beneficial resource in courting improvement.

One who reveals extra empathy than the normal character is referred to as an empath. These folks often have a higher degree of accuracy at the same time as identifying emotions on a few different individual's face. Additionally, they'll be extra willing than specific people to apprehend sentiments early and choose such feelings to be more potent. Empaths are prone folks who can examine one-of-a-kind human beings's emotions and mind.

Being an empath comes with many blessings. On the plus side, empaths generally make splendid pals. They have excellent listening abilties. They generally assist their buddies once they want them. They have large hearts and are giving. Also not unusual among empaths is a immoderate diploma of highbrow flair and friendliness. For empaths, some of the extreme developments that render them such amazing pals can be hard. Empaths frequently address other people's troubles as their personal. Even even as asked an excessive amount of, it is commonly hard for kids to set up limits autonomously and say nay.

Additionally, empaths frequently experience fatigue after being with others. Since introverts have a propensity to be empaths, they require a fine quantity of solitude to refuel. A 2011 look at famous a connection among social tension & strain in specifically empathetic people. People who are normally overly privy to person trends and persistent talk discover it difficult to sympathize amid crowds. Usually, being in nature makes them feel their excellent. It's vital to discover ways to keep away from devouring different human beings's sentiments and suffering and the way to center ourselves in frazzling environment that are not empathic nice if you need to live as an empath. The world might be a whole lot less complex to navigate after you grasp the fundamentals of self-protection, and your fitness & enjoy of properly-being may additionally even decorate.

Dr. Judith Orloff, the trailblazer in the mission, calls empaths "emotional sponges" who take inside the emotions and frustrations of the out of doors worldwide. In her e-book, she claims that empaths have very little filters that many humans use to protect themselves from overstimulation and cannot avoid taking in surrounding thoughts and emotions and impulses, whether or not or now not or now not tremendous or poor or a few component in amongst. Therapist Kim Egel, who practices in San Diego, elaborates similarly: "Empaths have an extended sensitivity to outdoor stimuli like sounds, sturdy personalities, and busy environments. They are very heartfelt and annoying humans who have robust emotions. Being an empath has numerous benefits. On the plus side, empaths frequently make top notch partners. They pay interest nicely. They frequently help pals once they need them. They have large hearts and are giving.

Additionally, empaths regularly own robust emotional intelligence and instinct. It may be difficult for empaths to address some of the essential difficulty trends that cause them to such super buddies. Since empaths enjoy what their pals are experiencing, they are vulnerable to severe poor emotions like fear or wrath. Empaths have the propensity to adopt other humans's troubles as their personal. Even whilst requested to do too much, they need to set limits and refuse requests.

Additionally, empaths often experience a experience of exhaustion after being amongst others. The majority of empaths are nerds, and that they need solitude time to recharge. According to a 2011 observe, there may be a connection among social tension and people who're notably empathetic. Since empaths are regularly particularly touchy to precise stimuli and regular speech, crowds may also moreover enjoy in particular oppressive. They often experience their tremendous emotions in natural settings.

1.2 History of Empathy

The phrase has fine been used for sort of a century, but its which means that has evolved drastically.

Today, there may be a incredible deal of debate regarding empathy development. However, maximum people are unaware that the term "empathy" modified into first delivered in 1908. Oddly sufficient, its actual definition grow to be quite the opposite of what we now understand empathy to entail.

"Empathy" turn out to be interpreted at the identical time as psychologists hooked up studies facilities and educational responsibilities to release psychology as a new vicinity. Only some generations ago, even as philosophers exploring the psyche began out to adopt in-lab research on belief and revel in, the ultra-contemporary have a have a take a look at had its beginnings. Psychologists needed to interpret medical words in German, as most of those labs have been positioned at German institutions.

Thus, in 1908, the English word "empathy" first originated as a rendition of the German Einfühlung, because of this "in feeling." Initially, empathy became greater about expressing one's assumed sentiments and actions approximately matters than it changed into approximately comprehending some different man or woman. Since the spectator projected their sensations of accomplishing earlier into the hill or architectural column, empathy defined how someone regarded a hill or form column as although it have been ascending. Similar to how site visitors positioned their internal feeling of motion onto the styles, precis strains may want to likely appear to be moving in a photograph. The satisfaction of artwork modified into perception to depend on empathy.

Psychologists commenced attempting out human beings's perceptual empathy and placed that humans regarded strains with acute angles as angry and contours heading upward as powerful and upbeat. Rebecca West, a author, referred to her exhilarating experience of growing with a bird because it arced through the air as "empathy," despite the reality that the word hadn't yet appeared in lots of dictionaries in 1928. Empathy lets in for the self to in truth come to be the pondered item.

American psychologists began out to expand the definition of empathy to embody comprehending other humans after discovering that it first of all had a classy value. To understand what every exceptional person is going through, one may furthermore, as an example, switch one's private recalled sentiments of depression onto that individual's sad look. Sociologists and psychologists looked at how empathy ought to help practitioners in better comprehending their sufferers inside the 1930s.

In the years following World War II, social psychologists began out out growing exams to determine a topic's compassion for others. Empathy permits one to effectively forecast every different individual's picks without tainting the ones predictions with one's own opinions. The belief that empathy has been the inventive translation of one's sentiments into devices vanished as it advanced to mean the functionality to well recognize some other individual's feelings & thoughts.

1.Three Types of Empaths

Do you usually typically tend to react emotionally earlier than wondering? Are you so sensitive to distinct people's sentiments that your frame responds to them as even though they will be your personal? You may be an empath, breaking facts! Continue analyzing to find out what it technique to be an empath and what kind of empath you're.

When you anticipate about empaths, you typically photograph human beings with heightened empathy: sensitivity to one of a kind human beings's thoughts and feelings. According to famous perception, empaths circulate past definitely comprehending those emotions and revel in things as though they were really taking vicinity. What if we knowledgeable you that it have become only one kind? What if someone knowledgeable you that human beings among us need to communicate with spirits, apprehend dreams, and talk with animals?

You might also name the guys in white jackets to p.C. Us up and take us to the chuckling manufacturing unit. The chemistry of empathy may additionally furthermore astound you, so please undergo with us.

We have located that there are 14 taken into consideration one in all a kind sorts of empaths. Although there is super overlap, anyone has a very particular set of research. It's a debatable hassle, so be skeptical of simply all and sundry who knows the precise style of types that exist.

Sensitive Empath

All empaths show off a diploma of more sensitivity to special people's feelings.

However, it's miles their excellent or sole empathic feature in emotional empaths. Some people also can take delivery of as real with that their empathy-based absolutely abilties stand on their private. Some humans could probable experience they will be losing out at the most interesting abilities related to other empath categories.

Telepathic Empath

Telepathic empaths take subjects to the following diploma due to the fact they may be able to examine one of a kind people's mind and emotions.

Telepathic empaths regularly "look at minds" through the usage of staring at body language like emotive empaths. It's difficult to determine if it denotes a higher degree of expertise or a distinct standpoint. The empath organization is break up on this trouble.

Physical Empath

Physical empaths assert that they're more sensitive than commonplace to others' bodily well-being. They can tell whether or not a few difficulty is wrong alongside aspect your physical properly-being thru manner of paying attention to others speak about their migraines and stomachaches.

Some human beings additionally mimic distinct humans's physical styles, little quirks, and unnoticeable behaviors. Do you recognise the manner whenever you examine anybody else yawning, you would love to yawn too? For physical empaths, the sensation is comparable however an lousy lot greater excessive.

Psychometric Empath

Psychometric empaths can also moreover check someone's connection to a difficulty or region. A psychometric empath can enjoy the love and disappointment you revel in while you gaze at a portrait of a deceased loved one or the memories sparked at the same time as you hold a prized relic.

Some assert that they may be capable of link with vain gadgets psychically on their very own, with out the useful resource of every other person. Once more, reviews disagree on whether or not or no longer or no longer it indicates that psychometric empathy is more potent or whether or not or no longer they may be simply uniquely using their abilities.

Molecular Empath

The inner maximum plausible degree of resonance is concept to exist among Molecular Empaths and distinctive human beings. It's doubtful if it takes place at the same molecular diploma that we component out at the same time as discussing physics.

In either case, molecular empaths often get insights into some other individual's real nature—their center self, stripped of all the layers of selfishness we accumulate through the years.

Some of the tips they deliver may want to probably marvel you.

Animal or Fauna Empath

Animal empaths are specially expert at deciphering the emotions of our animal friends.

It is rarely a Doctor Dolittle situation, after all. The posture, thoughts-set, and motions of an animal, similarly to what they display concerning the animal's inner existence, are deeply perceptible to animal/fauna empaths. These are as smooth to understand to animal empaths as terms. Gives "Duck Tales" a present day day which means.

Akin to cats, now which you factor out it, certain fauna empaths might also intentionally revel in the companionship of animals to that of human beings, on the equal time as others can also tolerate us.

Flora or Plant Empath

Plant empaths might also furthermore select out up at the energy of flora, similar to how an animal empath may additionally moreover feel the happiness of severa animals.

It is a unique gift that plant empaths can also additionally find out difficult to explain due to the versions in how people and plant life recognize cognizance (or the plant identical).

Plant empaths might be placing the framework for his or her immoderate human nicely-being, for the motive that the blessings of being concerned for flowers are properly documented.

Geomantic or Earth Empath

Such empaths are acutely aware about changes inside the planet's bodily composition.

Some assert that they may be capable of sense the struggling due to volcanoes and wildfires and perhaps even foresee them. Similar to plant empaths, it is unknown how the Earth's recognition is transferred into the range of human feelings.

Indigo Empath

Indigo empaths are involved with morality and distinctive function, now not to be stressed through azure children, who're simply different creatures. An indigo empath is inclined to understand negative faith once they see it.

They are actually interested in those who behave morally uprightly, stressful extra approximately a person's better than their niceness. Very one-of-a-type.

Intuition Empath

Through reputedly magical leaps of reasoning, intuitive empaths discern the truth of a scenario.

They can acquire facts apparently out of skinny air and experience emotions and emotions. You recognize the ones those who, whilst getting into a domestic for the primary time, at once recognize which kitchen cabinet to search for? Yes, it empaths with intuition.

The difference amongst this and Luke Skywalker is not one million moderate-years.

Precognitive Empath

Predictive or precognitive empaths become aware about the possibilities of a scenario.

The result is the equal if they are able to foretell the destiny due to a high-quality psychic potential or recognize patterns and choose out the most probable state of affairs. Don't declare they failed to alert you because of the truth that they understand what must arise.

Medium or Psychic Empath

They assert that a medium or psychic empath has an innate interest of the afterlife.

They can enjoy extrasensory strength from the non secular realm and located it to use to draw judgments approximately troubles within the bodily worldwide. Depending at the empath's ideals, they will employ a sure technique. There are in all likelihood no longer many atheist empaths round.

Dream Empath

Dream empaths have terrific memory and dream interpretation skills.

To this form of empath, the significance of what our synapses talk to us while we sleep is as obvious because the alphabet. Dream empaths are possibly the problem of the biblical account of Joseph, and modern-day-day reincarnation can assist us access the identical shape of intuitive facts.

Heyoka Empath

In the languages of the Dakota and Lakota Native Americans, "heyoka" method "holy clown" or "spiritual idiot."

Heyoka empaths are belief to be the maximum powerful and unusual type, serving as a soul mirror to others near them to assist of their improvement.

The Heyoka's unconventional way of living reasons people to reevaluate their conceptions of what is actual and imaginary. That man or woman stirring up your emotions on social media can be a Heyoka empath supporting you out.

1.Four Psychology and Mechanism of Empathy

Empaths normally pass over some factor in their life, which incorporates affection, admiration, a feel of belonging, and compassion; as a end end result, they choice for others to have something they pass over inside the hopes of receiving it in pass returned. Even the most worn-out and sad empaths will go to any amount to uplift others.

Science also has an impact. In her 2017 studies, Dr. Judith Orloff lists five clinical theories that shed similarly mild on empathy.

Mirror Neuron System

Electromagnetic Field

Emotional Contagiousness

Increased Dopamine Sensitivity

Synesthesia

Mirror Neuron System

Researchers have decided thoughts cells which is probably at once in control of compassion. Empaths can mimic the research and emotions of others due to the truth to mirror neurons. For example, empaths may also moreover revel in ache if a person is depressed. Sociopaths, psychopaths, and narcissists, in evaluation, hand, are said to lack empathy. They aren't capable of experience sympathy for absolutely everyone. These humans's underactive mirror neuron device is why they behave this way. In maximum instances, an event that takes region to someone else triggers reflect neurons. If we're disenchanted, harm, or pleased, others without replicate neurons might not sense something for us.

Electromagnetic Fields

The advent of electromagnetic fields with the aid of the thoughts and coronary coronary heart inside the body is a few different scientific discovery. People's feelings and emotions are transmitted through these organs. Empaths are frequently vulnerable to this stimulation, making them experience compelled and stressed. The Earth and the sun additionally effect emotional reactions.

Emotional Contagion

We need to be aware about the human beings we spend time with at the equal time as we're capable of enjoy everyone else's moods and feelings all spherical us. Spending time with negative people can drain your powerful electricity. Being an empath makes it simple to experience different people's feelings. A individual is taken into consideration to have empathy, as an instance, in the event that they see every other person yawning. That is visible as a deliver of emotional contagion. Many people will yawn in response to as a minimum one character. Most human beings are aware about contagion; as an example, if one toddler starts offevolved to cry, the other babies inside the nursery can also even weep. Relationships and expertise what the opportunity may be experiencing at any particular time rely upon the capacity to take a look at people's moods. Empaths want to isolate themselves from every body's horrific emotions; consequently try to companion themselves with effective humans as a substitute.

Chapter 7: Characteristics, Highs & Lows Of Being Empath

When it refers to emotions, empaths are receptive, finely-tuned gadgets. They are a great deal much less probable to intellectualize their emotions and revel in the whole thing, on occasion extra. Their revel in of the world is filtered thru impulse. Empaths are notable listeners, herbal givers, and spiritually aware humans. Empaths have hearts in case you want one. They are the best caretakers inside the worldwide, there for you via thick and thin.

2.1 Self-Assessment for Being Empath

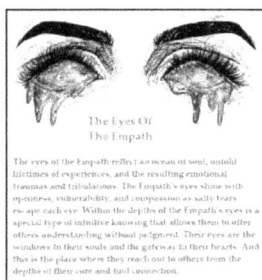

The Eyes Of The Empath

The eyes of the Empath reflect an ocean of soul, untold lifetimes of experiences, and the resulting emotional traumas and tribulations. The Empath's eyes shine with openness, vulnerability, and compassion as salty tears escape each eye. Within the depths of the Empath's eyes is a special type of intuitive knowing that allows them to offer others understanding without judgment. Their eyes are the windows to their souls and the gateway to their hearts. And this is the place where they reach out to others from the depths of their care and find connection.

Empaths are recognized for having a eager information of your attitude. Some people are capable of regulating people's emotions without doing so. Others, but, can also additionally land up being angst-sucking sponges for higher or worse, much like myself and plenty of my clients. It commonly takes precedence over the fantastic capacity to take in high-quality emotions & all this is cute. If empaths are near love and peace, their our our bodies soak up and increase. However, negativity often appears overwhelming and unsightly. They are, therefore, smooth prey for energy vampires, whose tension or wrath can harm empaths. They also can furthermore put on weight to act as a buffer and a cover. They are greater liable to negativity at the same time as they will be thin.

An incapacity to well known the motive of overeating. Additionally, the delicacy of an empath may be worrying in love relationships. Many are however unmarried because of the fact they have not determined the manner to barter their cohabitation dreams with a partner.

Stressful sentiments can cause numerous bodily signs and signs and symptoms and signs and signs and symptoms in empaths, beginning from exhaustion to agoraphobia, further to anxiety attacks, melancholy, meals and drug binges, and intercourse binges. You do now not constantly must enjoy very emotional to be empathic. Kindness lets in set me free, igniting my compassion, vibrancy, and enjoy of the staggering now that I can heal myself and prevent tackling civilization's ills. Take the quiz beneath to discover if you're an emotional empath.

You can inquire within:

Have I been accused of being too sensitive or emotionally unstable?

Do my feelings get damage resultseasily?

Do I want time to get better psychologically after being spherical many humans?

Do loud noises, robust odors, or excessive conversation make me worried?

Do I decide to force someplace just so I may additionally moreover go away every time I want?

Do I take pride in emotional ingesting?

Am I involved that near relationships must consume me?

You are at least in element empathic in case you answered "yes" to as a minimum one to three of those questions. You will apprehend you have were given got observed your emotional type in case you reply "yes" to extra than three questions. The first step in the path of handling your emotions instead of continuously drowning in them is admitting which you're an empath. Maintaining recognition of empathy will enhance each relationships and self-care.

2.2 Benefits and Drawbacks of Empathy

You also can understand the benefits and disadvantages of being an empath based on how a bargain you have got observed out you're one. The truth that it is probably a great load to go through due to the outside power and thoughts you are encircled by seems to be one of the drawbacks, as we have got already referred to. However, the bulk of stuff in lifestyles has each advantages and downsides. Being surrounded via using the use of such emotions can be top notch and beneficial in numerous strategies.

The benefits and drawbacks cannot be in truth incredible due to the fact they'll be regularly entangled. Listeners are empaths. They are commonly thrilled and extroverted, but they will be the entirety but joy. Not to be forgotten is the heyoka empath, famend for cracking jokes even as you least count on it. As empaths are liable to mood swings, their journey is probably of soft happiness and emotional sorrow. It's due to the truth they will be no longer continually in control in their thoughts. Empaths may additionally revel in temper swings that shift as speedy as turning a turn on and stale when they can't distinguish amongst their non-public emotions and thoughts and those of others. Being an empath also can result in terrible emotions together with despair, strain, anxiety, panic, and grief, in reality as wonderful ones. You may be experiencing extraordinary human beings's ache whilst having any have an impact on over those sentiments. It's a appreciably hard scenario that one person should not address.

Compassion is wanted in this sort of situation. Being left by myself also can damage one's mental and bodily health; due to this, empaths should have as a minimum one person they're capable to show to at the same time as the ones temper swings strike. Find each person you can depend upon while existence becomes too much for you, whether or not or now not it is a colleague, a associate, or a family member. Whoever you stumble upon, make sure to permit them to realise that every one you without a doubt need is empathy—the capability to enjoy sympathy without passing judgment on you. It should resource on your restoration from the ones attempting instances.

Except for those who have undertaken their adventures of self-discovery and self-popularity, most empaths are ignorant of their inner techniques. They are unaware that they'll be experiencing some other person's emotions as despite the fact that they have been their very non-public. It might also reason a whole lot of feelings, which includes uncertainty, specifically if some element grow to be terrific one second and dreadful the following. The ride includes information their empathetic connection.

An empath reveals it less hard to suppress feelings and sensations than others. They try to do the whole lot they may to avoid being bombarded with terrific humans's sentiments and feelings. As a stop stop end result, people regularly withdraw and boom numbing behaviors.

The downside is that they'll land up locking up their inner emotions or erecting such excessive boundaries that they in no manner permit all and sundry else in. It can be adverse to everybody, now not genuinely empaths, because the more the ones sentiments and feelings collect indoors you, the extra power they have. They in the end normally tend to erupt, which could cause vast harm to the empath and absolutely everyone close by. It ought to probable bring about a disorderly atmosphere, a intellectual or emotional fall apart, or perhaps illness.

Honest communication is a preference, but it's miles a powerful tool for healing.

The Drawbacks of Empathy

Some of these can also qualify as blessings based mostly on how you are taking them. You'll see how brief this list is compared to the amount of blessings. It is due to the fact having empathy may be a blessing if you apprehend the way to apply it.

Easily Overwhelmed

It's been introduced up in advance than, but being an empath likely has this as its fundamental downside. It is possible to be overpowered with the useful resource of the feelings and feelings of others round you in crowded locations. Sometimes, regardless of most effective one extra man or woman in the room, you'll probable enjoy this. Due to this, no longer some thing ought to be stored indoors.

Addictive Personalities

Empaths frequently try and keep away from or clean out off specific human beings's emotions. As a result, humans once in a while flip to addictive such things as intimacy, alcohol, and drugs. You might not constantly need to run from the ones gadgets in case you manipulate to protect your strength and self. Instead, you'll be capable to take care of them successfully.

Devastation of Media

Some empaths absolutely avoid the media. Even reviewing a newspaper appears too tough for the motive that they are capable of intensely feel one-of-a-kind humans's feelings. The global is a cruel place.

Quick Picker of Mental & Physical Illness

Considering your competencies's power, it would rise up even in case you do not interact with the opportunity individual. No one definitely wants to bear such type of struggling.

Being Negative with Lies & Hidden Secrets

It might be difficult to apprehend and experience these gadgets, in particular in case you cannot again them up with evidence. To stop often experiencing this, try to be within the business enterprise of like-minded others.

Homeless person

Empaths are tendencies to roam. We often start to feel normal in places we previously loved after a certain period has surpassed.

We are forced to discover the massive, uncharted universe through way of our instinct. It makes us never content to live in a single vicinity however moreover makes us great tourists.

Benefits of Empathy

We cited the alternatively excessive drawbacks. We may also additionally now observe the reasons for why having empathy is a present. Please be affected person with me due to the truth there are plenty of factors to bear in mind.

Natural Healers

Empaths are innate healers who can deal with emotional, environmental, bodily, animal, and wonderful ailments. They can collect it the usage of their voice, draw near, and originality. The reason why most empaths pick out a career in recuperation is that they may be actually interested in it.

Even despite the fact that an empath also can discover crowds difficult, they often create a decent-knit network for themselves. An empath turns into immensely dedicated and being concerned after they connect to someone. Because we do not need to allow the best ones to go, we keep firmly to our cherished ones.

We all recognize this, but empaths have a loopy amount of love. Said their hearts are larger than others. It's difficult to faux the ones sensations whilst crushed by way of way of them.

If you are taking be aware of that intestine feeling, it simply is quite effective, I even have a strong feeling you may take over the area. Since my intuition has in no way been wrong and I'm an empath, I'm looking to pay more hobby to it. If it hasn't already, pay attention to your sixth experience considering it may rescue you from dangers that would stand up.

Extraordinary Senses

We additionally own extremely good senses and a very sturdy intuition. Not really feelings and feelings are intensified. You might also additionally characteristic being an empath to the truth that you revel in a significant style of sensations with substantially extra intensity than humans near you. We can greater completely apprehend our meals, drinks, flower, vital oils, touches, and other topics due to the fact we've stronger senses. Although they'll weigh down us, they have got the potential to shop lives. You can also additionally marvel, how? Well, in case you cognizance on sprucing a specific revel in, like the scent, you might be able to stumble upon illness or lack of existence in nature, human beings, or unique residing topics. Although we have formerly stated that bearing the burden of various human feelings is hard and that we're vulnerable to lows, there can be additionally the alternative give up of the emotional spectrum. Great highs additionally occur to us. Most empaths surely have a profound zest for lifestyles, and we experience delight intensely even as doing so.

Extremely Creative

Empaths are drastically innovative humans! I've already stated this, however it deserves its difficulty. We each assume and have a look at the arena in precise techniques. Our studies, times, and possibilities are also revolutionary factors of our lives. Now, you have were given actually had the unfortunate revel in of hearing that your way of questioning and doing is inaccurate, however it's miles a strength all your own.

Don't permit someone to thieve your tremendous ingenuity; alternatively, permit it shine brightly. We can not be duped, but one more drawback is a fantastic. We are adept at decoding others' emotions, feelings, and mind. As a end result, we will apprehend while a person is dishonest, desires assist, or has a terrible concept.

Interpret Non-Verbal Clues

Empaths excel at deciphering nonverbal and emotional clues. It's a knowledge that exists everywhere. We can also even sense the needs of others who can't communicate verbally, which include flowers and animals, in addition to the frame and newborns, manner to our eager senses.

Desire to Improve the arena

Most empaths have a robust preference to enhance the area. There's no need to ever be embarrassed approximately this preference. This planet can also advantage from many changes, and we have to do on every occasion we're capable of. Already, too many human beings are final their eyes. Together, allow's try to right the wrongs in our network. Given our attraction to the area, we must regulate it. We belong to the herbal global. It can also convey calm and luxury and is one of the greatest techniques to de-stress. Some human beings might view this as extra of a drawback, however it's miles exquisite that we will refuel on our non-public. We require a specific quantity of by myself to recharge. We are self-aware because of this, that is excellent, in my view.

2.Three Characteristics of Empaths

What makes someone an empath more essential than what they do? If you are an empath, you have were given a better reason on this for the purpose that it is a part of your difficult-compelled nature. Many empaths are ignorant of their huge effect on the world if they're capable of allow their specific capacity glow via and encourage others. Here are a few traits and caution indicators that you could pick out out out with in case you're curious approximately what precisely an empath is and very own herbal empathic talents. It is a skills that allows you to comprehend others' feelings and thoughts out of doors your mindset. You recall subjects and movements more drastically in case you're an empath. You absorb and interpret feelings as even though they had been a part of your personal enjoy. Your pain or delight is a person else's satisfaction or ache. You're probable to reveal off a number of the ones trends in case you're an empath:

Highly Sensitive

You frequently get maintain of grievance for being too sensitive. It is because of how effortlessly you might be impacted via what they expect or do. You can infer meanings from what they do not say after they communicate or do a little component. Because of this sensitivity, you may be at risk of factors that don't damage nicely-adjusted people.

You take notable care in what you do and say because of the excessive level of sensitivity.

This sample always effects in self-restraint dispositions. You wind up over-personalizing your self to win over the area.

There are plenty of troubles that include the exercising of hiding your real emotions.

Accumulate the Energy of Other People

You may be having a notable day and feeling upbeat even as you visit Coffee shops and sit down down with a own family who, unknowingly to you, has these days out of place without a doubt one in every of its own family. There is silence. They're all quietly taking part in their espresso. Gradually, the euphoria you once felt begins offevolved to disappear, and melancholy takes its place. Even when you have no justification for feeling depressed, it despite the fact that takes vicinity to you as rapid due to the fact the circle of relatives leaves the Coffee shop and walks up; your despair vanishes. You had without a doubt engulfed them.

Introverted

Being shy isn't just like having introverted. On the alternative hand, introverts get exhausted once they spend too much time with different human beings and price their on my own time. A shy man or woman may additionally moreover want to loathe being on my own and experience avoided for missing human interplay. An introvert has a employer sense of self and remains dependable to it, in comparison to a person shy with self-inhibiting inclinations. Introverted people are greater willing to be empaths than extroverted human beings. They do now not avoid all human interaction, however they commonly have a propensity to interact with humans in my view or in small numbers.

Highly Intuitive

An empath's intestine intuition is one in all their only tools. They possess the functionality to hit upon a state of affairs's actual essence. It makes gambling video games to an empath a piece hard. Your deceit can be exposed to them proper away. As an empath, you often experience someone's right individual whilst you first meet them. You are always aware about your environment and can hit upon risk. Since you're an entire lot an awful lot much less inclined to be taken gain of, this expertise is surely one of the key benefits of being an empath.

Overwhelmed with the aid of Relations

In conventional partnerships, the significance of time spent together is pressured. Because they normally take hold of onto their accomplice's emotions and confuse them for their very personal, empaths can't flourish on this shape of courting. It isn't alleged to argue that empaths are incapable of dating. However, it's miles essential to dismantle the conventional framework of a connection. For example, they will have a space in their very non-public in which they will pass on the identical time as the urge to be via themselves arises, and their spouses ought to be know-how of them.

Difficult to Process Emotions

Most human beings pay near interest to their emotions. Whether at instances of satisfaction or depression, it moves all of sudden. They have brief emotional reactions as well. An empath gets the time to realise the emotions they are experiencing at the moment. For instance, depression may not hit you right away if some element awful takes place. They will to begin with try and make revel in of the occasion with the aid of again and again going over the specifics, and after that, melancholy will start to boil up internal of them. They have so robust emotional capacities. Thus, they revel in everything absolutely, whether or no longer it's miles happiness or sorrow.

Loving Nature

The majority of empaths are cushty while near nature. No specific workout replenishes their equilibrium as well as being encircled with the resource of the natural international, whether or not or now not or not it's miles the daytime caressing their frame, the rain pattering on them, or getting a deep breath of glowing air. They experience a strong experience of kinship with nature. A walk across an open region below the celebs could be one of the restorative movements for an empath going via a tsunami of feelings.

Deep Senses

The senses of an empath are distinctly superior. They can encounter even the smallest scent, see into shadows, pay hobby the faintest noise, and experience severa sensations. They are masters at recognizing the little topics, manner to their higher senses. Empaths appear to be conscious of factors that extremely good human beings may want to generally neglect. Because of this, individuals often excel at occupations that require cautious announcement and an hobby inside the precis.

Generous

An empath is the maximum unselfish shape of person there may be. They can help while not having some component. They are keen to head above and above to help. For example, an empath's coronary coronary heart is torn when they come across a terrible person and witness their misery. They desire to discover a manner to get them off the streets further to feeding them. Most humans within the global are detached to and irritated by means of way of slum dwellers. We can wager that empaths carry out a big detail in assisting the region's avenue kids and distinct inclined individuals.

Creative

Empaths regularly have first-rate imaginations. The type of feelings children are constantly feeling allows with this. Their revolutionary spirit is plain in almost each vicinity in their lives, together with their houses, individuals of the circle of relatives, delicacies, and—most significantly—their careers. A career in the arts is in all likelihood to obtain success for an empath. They have large potential to create paintings through tune, performing, or filmmaking. They often show off their feelings in reality and are adept at as it want to be taking pictures the emotions of others.

People Driven via You

An empath is willing to withdraw from society if ignorant of their unique talent. Instead of being in social conditions and going via all feasible feelings, they may alternatively retreat and be protected. Because of this, the overall public can also expand a terrible opinion of them. However, others may be drawn to an empath if they may be self-conscious and aware of their capability to take within the electricity round them. People are conscious that empaths very own excellent ability for comprehending people and assisting them in overcoming their problems.

2.Four Comparison of Empaths, Psychics, and Highly Sensitive Individuals

Although pretty sensitive people and empaths almost appear like studying from the identical net internet web page, the two range in some methods. You ought to first realise that being an empath or very touchy are not incompatible developments. Both of these are concurrently manageable. The following are some distinctions between empaths and extremely touchy human beings.

Empaths

A man or woman with the ideal ability to understand special humans's emotions and sensations as though they'll be their non-public without even striving is referred to as an empath. They have a protected sensitivity to the energies which can be all round them. When an empath enters a room and is going next to someone silently grieving, they will feel the frustration and revel in it as their personal. Because they cannot distinguish amongst their personal emotions and people of others, an empath ignorant of their potential may additionally furthermore revel in extreme conflict.

To determine in case you are an empath, ask the subsequent questions to yourself: Can you via manner of a few manner perceive people? Do you confuse specific humans's emotions in your private on the equal time as you experience them? Are you capable of anticipate similarly to exceptional people? When you first meet a person, do your sentiments shift? Do you ever query your codependency, neuroticism, or maybe sanity?

Are you able to parent minds? Being able to feel one-of-a-kind human beings's electricity may be super, but at the disadvantage, it can be tough whilst the ones energies are of a horrible type, particularly if the empath in difficulty is unaware of their ability. Empaths are innate, not decided. Their skills are inherited features which can be a part of their DNA and are frequently exceeded down through the generations. It implies which you can't learn how to be an empath. Whether you are or aren't an empath. If you're an empath, you are continuously willing to digest the emotions and electricity of different human beings.

Empaths often specific their emotions and are more aware of their surroundings than themselves. Empaths can also forget their very very own unique dreams due to it. Empaths are often non-violent and non-aggressive people. They function the mediator the bulk of the time. Empaths have an uncommon, uneasy experience in any region or situation that is chaotic or unbalanced. If they stumble upon a warfare of terms, they will attempt to clear up it as speedy as viable or live out of it actually. An empathic is probable to experience irritated if any awful language or profanity is used of their protection because of his lack of energy of will or discipline.

Due to their many certainly one among a type expressive temperaments, empaths have a sturdy interest in a large form of music. Others is probably confused through how empaths can hook up with one kind of music for a couple of minutes in advance than switching to each distinctive. Empaths cautiously take a look at the wording of songs. Words have a sturdy, horrific impact on human beings, in particular if the music is pertinent to their present instances or cutting-edge enjoy. It is usually recommended for an empath to experience track without accompanying lyrics in these times to save you scary their emotional country.

Psychics

The utilization of psychics within the media and films is pervasive. But what's the real definition of a psychic? The power hassle of a region, character, vicinity/constructing, or object may be tuned into with the useful resource of a psychic. Additionally, they will pick out up on past, present, and capability destiny traits. The auric or magnetic area of someone, area, or element may additionally provide psychics impressions and telepathically. Since they may find it instinctively, they seldom lease Spirit energy to get psychic information about others. The Para physical or spiritual senses of a psychic, together with clairvoyance, clairaudience, or wonderful spiritual skills noted later on this e-book, are how they reap facts. Psychic growth also can help with a choice of factors, inclusive of creating lifestyles alternatives, locating out of area gadgets, transferring, and enhancing one's stage of consciousness.

Psychic Empaths

Different kinds of empaths specialize mainly fields of psychic art work. The capability to understand the strength and vibration of the ground is called geomancy. This functionality may be used for dousing, locating water underground, or forecasting coming close to intense climate. The psychic know-how of psychometrics permits an empath to acquire impressions from severa objects. The police will from time to time hire this to remedy bizarre or violent instances. Another first-rate capability is known as Clair consciousness, wherein the empath is acquainted with exactly what steps to take or what to do in any given situation, especially in a disaster or an emergency.

They also can behave with truth, tranquility, and peace, encouraging the ones round them to do the same. As a psychic capabilities called mediumship, most empaths can understand and communicate with spirits. Some human beings can remodel energy and heal via sensing the signs and symptoms and signs and symptoms and symptoms of others.

They can also help others in overcoming emotional trauma. While some empaths can have interaction with animals, others can do the equal for nature. Another uncommon knowledge that psychic empaths very own is the capability to are looking ahead to drawing close to catastrophes or tragedies. Empaths, as formerly indicated, are blessed with crucial capabilities, but they frequently pay a great charge for these. They regularly face judgment and misunderstanding. They now and again moreover pay hobby insulting, even disdainful, comments on their statements. Empaths is probably greater sensitive to their environment, that could result in physical upsets and remarkable allergic reactions which may be difficult for ordinary scientific medical doctors to find out.

Even despite the fact that their abilities and talents are very critical, they'll be now not Different sorts of empaths who specialize particularly fields of psychic paintings. The capacity to perceive the electricity and vibration of the floor is called geomancy. This capability may be used for dousing, finding water underground, or forecasting coming near to shut to extreme weather. The psychic capacity of psychometrics allows an empath to accumulate impressions from numerous gadgets. The police will once in a while utilize this to clear up weird or violent crimes. Another high-quality capability is called Clair consciousness, wherein the empath knows precisely what steps to take or what to do in any given state of affairs, specially in an emergency or a disaster. They may also moreover behave with fact, tranquility, and peace, encouraging the ones round them to do the same. As a psychic talent referred to as mediumship, a few empaths can recognize and communicate with spirits. Some human beings can remodel energy and heal with the useful resource of sensing the signs and symptoms of others. They also can assist others in overcoming emotional trauma. While a few empaths can have interaction with animals, others can do the identical with nature. Another uncommon knowledge that psychic empaths private is the capacity to are looking ahead to drawing near catastrophes or tragedies. Empaths, as previously indicated, are blessed with critical abilities, but they frequently pay a extremely good charge for the ones. They regularly face judgment and misconception. They occasionally moreover pay attention insulting, even disdainful, comments on their statements. Empaths is probably more sensitive to their environment, that could cause physical upsets and weird hypersensitive reactions which may be hard for everyday scientific clinical docs to find out. They are wonderful of their competencies and talents but now not all-understanding. Knowing that their skills won't usually be at their fantastic or that they might not constantly be able to remedy all of humanity's illnesses and illnesses, Their skills may not continuously feature at their superb, and they won't be capable of treatment every human ailment and infection.

Being Psychic Empath

How do if what you are experiencing or getting is genuinely psychic, logical, or in reality whole creativeness? Is one of the most usually requested concerns about psychic improvement? Imagination and reasoning are especially exceptional from psychic or "intuitive" sensations. These impressions are generally unplanned or sudden sentiments, emotions, mind, photos, and sometimes smells or tastes. They can appear in severa techniques, which includes instinct, foresight, visions, and knowledge of the beyond. A person might also additionally moreover sense a shift of their Workplace, which incorporates imminent layoffs, after which test that 10 human beings had been fired the subsequent morning. It might be a psychic perception or a message from our instinct. These sensations come to us via our Para bodily senses, or the five "clairs," which I shall communicate inside the next financial disaster, in choice to the use of our five physical senses.

Psychic Impressions can appear in any of the subsequent techniques: chronic, unsightly sensation, surprising interruption, surprising or impromptu interference along facet your normal manner of wondering or being. Contradicting your ideals, as an instance, you can suddenly sense the desire to booze on a number one date even if you're easy and do now not use alcohol. You check your date later, a bartender through profession. Strong feeling or memory attached. Not in any respect inspired or activated with the useful resource of your environment out of doors. Reoccurring visible numerals and symbols like 1111 or 1212 Temperature and shade trade, you'll have non-prevent psychic impulses that malicious program you. They also can marvel you and derail your intellectual technique. For instance, consider jogging at your table entering statistics at the same time as a image of your childhood exceptional buddy crying includes mind . Even when you have not spoken to her in a long term, you unexpectedly want to Contact her due to the reality you cannot withstand the impulse. You get onto Facebook and find out from her reputation publish that her mother has exceeded away. Here is an instance of the way a intellectual effect have to appear to draw our hobby. No out of doors stimulus would probably intrude along side your normal highbrow approach or capability to pay hobby.

Logic regularly follows a specific line of reasoning or pattern and is sparked via ecological factors or outside events. Similar to daydreaming, it truly is fast abandoned, so is our creativeness. Information conveyed via the use of psychic sensations is a long manner extra hard to ignore or reject. What kind of knowledge are you able to advantage from a psychic affect? Psychic impressions can also furthermore offer facts approximately an character, area, detail, or animal, which consist of preceding connections, Family lifestyles records, critical turning points, Potential future directions, present-day situations, recent changes in existence, interests/hobbies, karmic styles or soul teachings. Your mind want to stay smooth, centered, and unbiased even as you refine your instinct. Your thoughts turns into plenty tons much less cluttered through meditation, making you wiser and greater intuitive.

Highly Sensitive Individual

Swiss psychiatrist Carl Jung studied the important psychic dispositions that constructed up the communal unconscious at the start of the twentieth century. He recognized "innate sensitiveness," a tremendous of remarkable sensitivity, as one of the tendencies. According to Jung, positive people's intrinsic sensitivity makes them much more likely to be adversely suffering from demanding or upsetting adolescence events, which makes it harder for them to modify and cope as adults. Events that depart a long-lasting impact on sensitive people are in no way virtually forgotten. Some stay influential, and such activities can significantly effect a person's intellectual development. Carl G. Jung Becoming a mainly touchy person has benefits, in keeping with Jung, specially whilst there's a experience of serenity and equilibrium. He understood that being sensitive became now not a sign of a persona infection but have become frequently a splendid top notch that, beneath the right situations, may additionally additionally decorate one's tremendous of life. This severe sensitivity regularly outcomes in person improvement. However, the advantage usually becomes a amazing disadvantage even as hard and remarkable instances develop due to the truth quiet attention is distracted by means of the usage of unexpected consequences. However, no longer some thing will be similarly from the reality than considering this heightened sensitivity a disordered character trait in and of itself. If that were the case, we would ought to classify spherical 25 percent of human beings as fantastic.

Carl G. Jung Numerous exclusive studies later installation Jung's findings, and one mainly, Dr. Aron, has substantially brought to the data concerning HSPs. She is a pioneer in investigating sensitivity making use of (MRI) magnetic resonance imaging to check what transpires in extraordinarily touchy human beings' brains. Dr. Aron started out reading innate sensitivity in 1991. She centered her studies on three regions of interest: introverts' higher sensitivity, a super percent of newborns' inherent responsiveness, and biologists' observations of a comparable function in severa animal species. In a 2006 e-book for the Magazine of Jungian Theory and Practice, Dr. Aron states, "Whatever its eventual call, I even have come to be urged to try to assemble a diploma to emerge as aware about and check humans with this selection. According to Dr. Aron, immoderate sensitivity, moreover referred to as sensory-processing sensitivity, is an intrinsic high-quality that reasons people to pay closer attention to info and take in facts greater very well. But this concept does not cowl the extent to which those sensitivities are expressed.

Chapter 8: Relations & Work Life Of Empaths

Like exclusive people, empaths need to revel in at domestic of their Workplace to be content material and properly. Empaths is probably a terrific deal a great deal less resilient to distress than distinct human beings, making it more difficult to swing over again from annoying situations without being tired or sick because of their artwork. The traits of empaths are creators, innovators, visionaries, artists, and feelers. We navigate the Workplace whilst keeping an eye on the broader photo. Corporate or popular administrative center environments may be too constraining for us because of the truth we frequently think out of doors the sphere, but as quickly as our skills are used, employment may be profitable, invigorating, and thrilling.

Empaths flourish in the proper workplace putting. A career that fits our personalities can also additionally encourage us, spark our creativity, and growth our passion and strength. An empath's beneficiant heart is also happy with the useful aid of the records that we've got made a difference, regardless of how minor. But, the wrong career can drain us definitely and reason highbrow and bodily issues because of stress and emotional extra. In this financial ruin, I'll offer guidelines for deciding on the appropriate line of work on your capabilities and sensory requirements. Being comfortable at paintings is crucial for an empath's fitness because we spend quite a few time there.

three.1 Succeeding inside the Workplace

Our degree of consolation is encouraged through manner of three critical factors: the importance of our undertaking, the strength of others round us, and the power of the bodily surroundings. Analyze your gift function concerning the ones elements and begin to formulate improvement thoughts.

Important Work

Empaths discover pleasure in challenge good sized artwork which fits their sensitivity. We pick out to assume that our moves have superior the area or the lives of others. Anything from gardening to on foot a meals provider to operating inside the helping professions may also qualify as such. Though nice days is probably hard in any employment, the situation should crucially sense instinctively correct in our bodies and not drain our energy.

I keep in mind myself lucky to have determined employment as a speaker, writer, and desired practitioner that I am enthusiastic about. Like several wonderful empaths, I just like the use of my talents and being of assist to others. We can constantly help our coworkers and one-of-a-type people, whether or not we are medical doctors, food servers, lawyers, or hair stylists. Every profession gains significance from this adorable manner of thinking. Let the elegance we love what we do, because of the truth the top notch Rumi advises. There are endless variations at the floor-kissed function. Work that is unpleasant or boring might be made more bearable with the resource of way of that specialize in humility and assisting others or the greater actual.

Follow the Instinct with Courage

Workplace pressure and risks are number one reasons of empath soreness. They battle to conform to destructive surroundings and are with out troubles brought about.

Empaths experience extreme tension while walking in jobs regarding normal purchaser interactions due to the reality they start to popularity more on the humans they'll be handling than the mission they're performing. Given it, choosing the fine professional direction for an empath is critical. Empaths generally excel in corporation-oriented and coffee-stress professions like schooling or remedy. Empaths are inquisitive about innovation, and that they desire running for themselves. Empaths are regularly referred to as "energy vampires" due to their amazing capacity to attract power from those near them.

People's Vibes in Your Environment

Our consolation degree at art work can be made or broken with the beneficial aid of our employers, colleagues, and workmates. Sensitive human beings have a lesser tolerance for politicking, conflict of terms, and loudness. Empaths might possibly come to be exhausted and harassed because of place of job turmoil that would exceptional annoy someone. Sensitive people feature higher in welcoming environments that recognize cooperation and generosity. A sensitive character is not a certainly high-quality in shape for immoderate-stress, competitive employment on Wall Street. We ideally want to experience cushty with our colleagues and executives, however a administrative center that allows empaths is in reality unique. Finding precise employees with whom empaths may also be part of is a more viable intention. We do quality as we trap positive earth angels who do, despite the reality that no longer all in a administrative center may be first-rate or recognize our values.

In times of tension and exhaustion, supportive connections may be lifesaving. However, electricity scavengers are energetic all round us. Narcissists, wrath addicts, sufferers, passive-aggressiveness, ordinary talkers, and whiners are some of those vampires. Those vampires may be determined in any place of job, and being sucked with the aid of 1 influences our capability to function emotionally and physically at work. It's hard to break out from poisonous colleagues, subordinates, and bosses, which makes them in particular awful at art work. When we start to tackle everyone's toxicity, empaths could probable revel in fitness problems together with exhaustion, infection, ache, or an exacerbation of pre-gift illnesses. Remember the numerous coping mechanisms we referred to to prepare for depleting coworkers. I as soon as had an empath inform me, "I do my manner & float far from all people who intends a guilt enjoy or melodrama or who is a sleazebag or a moaner. The night time time shift is what I work to keep away from the regular gossip, useless small chat, and politics said an empath nurse approximately her approach. I can deliver my sufferers and my desired artwork my all at night time time. The lack of power may be decreased with the use of the ones system. Spending time with upbeat colleagues who can shield you in opposition to the greater destructive ones is likewise a superb idea.

Physical Space Energy

Each administrative center, staircase, and the constructing has a awesome vibe of its non-public. While some locations are encouraging, others aren't. Empaths have instead superior sensitivities that allow them to revel in the vibe of a physical surroundings. I advise you to pay attention to the vibe at art work to ensure it appears correct. Sometimes there may be residual strength from preceding tenants, fine or awful. Putting rose water inside the space will cleanse the vibe if you phrase that it seems peculiar. Although it is a useful approach for purifying a room, smoldering sage might probable cause smoke alarms to set off or disillusioned coworkers who might not be familiar with or uncomfortable with lively ritual cleaning.

Additionally, you could meditate on the Workplace—by myself or with like-minded colleagues—to fill it with soul power and clear out any toxicity or stagnation. You may also even rent a Feng shui expert who arranges fixtures, shrubs, reflect, and particular devices to create a harmonious setting. Empaths moreover respond to different factors which have an impact on how a bodily environment feels. These embody the shape of lighting, the quantity of noise and hobby, odors, the airflow, being close to colleagues, and the manque of privateness. Without home windows or beneath robust fluorescent lighting, empaths warfare. We additionally have a tendency to experience claustrophobic, both loads or a piece, who opt for a large personal region to shield ourselves from the strain of others. Compared to a peaceful, roomy, and ordered set, a hectic environment may be scary and draining.

A lot of nearby technological machine additionally can be taxing. Some empaths, which I communicate over with as "electro-sensitives," are mainly liable to it.

Laptops and cellular telephones emit electromagnetic waves that mess with the electromagnetic fields surrounding our minds and soul. The National Toxicology Program has these days proven a link among smartphone rays and mind and coronary heart cancers in mice. When I'm at paintings, one empath informed me that I attempt to hide the display screen as plenty as viable. Less applicable are large shows. I make the effort to take pauses at the same time as using the pc and try to limit my cellphone use.

Last however not least, the vibe of a workplace is drastically triggered with the useful resource of manner of the individuals there. Positive human beings provide brilliant electricity, while horrible ones produce terrible power. However, you can use flora, crystals, and religious artifacts to surround your Workplace in a peaceful cocoon, even in a hectic or tension-inducing surroundings.

Specific Profession for Empaths

Empaths excel in jobs that require creativity and customer support. The fine initiatives for humans with immoderate ranges of sensitivity are those that would because it ought to be painting an empath's dispositions inside the real global. HSPs (pretty sensitive humans) like assisting professions, inventive careers, and self-employment. To collect in work, they ought to make use of their sensitivity to its fullest. Low-strain professions are higher high-quality for them thinking about they'll be without issues encouraged with the aid of manner of the feelings of others round them, which include sufferers, customers, or coworkers.

Those in the scientific area, which include physicians, midwives, naturopaths, and lots of others.

Work within the arts, which include writing and portray.

Social or public provider education

Occupations artwork with animals, including pup professionals and animal sitters.

Having a venture with a nonprofit

Psychologists, counselors, therapists, rehabilitators, and special counseling and highbrow fitness experts

Positions to Avoid

Empaths, as we've got were given already hooked up, are proficient with the ability to absorb wonderful and terrible strength from the ones round them. Empaths consider that excessive-strain professions like marketing and advertising and income are hard and emotionally horrible. Customer interactions are in particular tough and psychologically draining for introverted empaths. Sensitive folks who perform in profits often describe feeling worn out and finding it tough to have interaction with people all day. The types of employment which can be least appropriate for empaths had been recognized through research on their nicely-being and intellectual health.

These positions encompass the ones in income, advertising and advertising and advertising and marketing, and retail, including strolling at a shop or promoting merchandise to make money for the industrial company.

Public individuals of the family positions in politics, at the side of manager and recruiter positions.

An empath will become overwhelmed at the same time as attractive with others and being close to them.

They save you that specialize in their paintings and placed all their hobby on certainly one of a type human beings.

Therefore, the occupations that allow empaths to consciousness extra in their power on themselves at the same time as running with out feeling overburdened are the finest for them.

Guidelines for Juggling Work and Life as an Empath

You will experience sure difficulties in the interest in case you are an empath.

Everyone wishes to carry out in a role that is a right suit for their abilities and character, but you want to be specifically careful on the identical time as accepting a activity since a toxic administrative center might also moreover brief make you physically, emotionally, and mentally unwell. Therefore, as an empath, do you choose out out the right career and be triumphant there? Empaths are emotional siphons that take at the anxiety of others and preserve it interior their our our bodies. I recognize how draining it could be because I am an empath myself. Here are a few clean strategies for empaths and all and sundry suffering with low depth at art work.

Create Energy Boundaries at Work

Develop a mental barrier at some point of the fringe of your table in an open area or a hectic place of work thru way of surrounding it with greenery or photographs of your family. Holy beads, crystals, or shielding stones also can create an electricity border, as can statues of Quan Yin, St. Francis, or Buddha. Additionally, taking periods for respite inside the restroom or, if you could, going for a walk inside the outdoor is vital. The utilization of noise-canceling earphones or headphones allows to block out undesirable noises like discussions. You can also image a glowing golden egg round your Workplace to ward off terrible energy and permit only top electricity through. Imagine being enclosed inner this golden egg, protected and strong. You may also additionally moreover rely upon the protecting cocoon that is created by all of those strategies. Even at the identical time as you do not have an impact on the complete Workplace, you could exchange the vibe inside the area round you. You may additionally additionally reduce emotional transmission with the aid of concentrating at the strong surroundings you create in area of the chaos and commotion spherical you. Your time at paintings will then appear considerably greater stable and extra a laugh.

Be Wary of Energy Vampires

In maximum instances, you could spoil off communication with an power succubus for your personal lifestyles or, a minimum of, restriction how a good deal time you percentage. Unfortunately, it isn't the case if you have to art work alongside them. Here, regulations end up important. You ought to strongly but in a well mannered way assert your self from the start of your art work relationship. Avoid carrying out trivial workplace gossip and decline invitations from poisonous coworkers to socialize. Put your health and tremendous of life earlier than artwork commitments and use your better energy self-protection strategies. Empaths who select to work with human beings or animals within the offerings vicinity must be conscious of how their paintings impacts their energy levels. For instance, speaking to a affected man or woman heading through a mainly tragic or difficult time of their lives can reason you to experience wiped out, drained, or even depressed in case you carry out as a therapist or psychologist. Schedule enough time to unwind and deal with your self beyond work, and consider to offer yourself a couple of minutes among customers or consultations to pay attention.

Distinction Between Home & Workplace

Create a habitual that establishes a top notch boundary among your business business enterprise and private lives in case you paintings a ways from domestic because of the truth you're an empath and susceptible to taking on different people's terrible electricity. You may be aware that you start to fear not pretty much your artwork problems however moreover about your coworkers, superiors, and clients. If you do no longer accumulate a way to "transfer off," you'll quickly revel in strain, tension, and melancholy. When it is time to complete the day's hobby, be cognizant of the exchange from artwork to home. Make a recurring that turns on you to shift your interest from your coworkers' and customers' goals in your pastimes and feelings. For instance, you could want to apply the remaining 15 minutes of the challenge to meditate or easy your workspace on the equal time as being attentive to a selected soundtrack or music. You may also additionally additionally make it a workout to touch a friend or family who continuously makes you experience more energized unexpectedly earlier than leaving the place of work or on the manner decrease returned home.

Consider How Your Work Can Benefit Others

It's no longer always viable to switch jobs or pursue a career within the place of your choice. If you cannot depart your contemporary employment because it isn't appropriate for you, keep in thoughts viewing your paintings from a brilliant angle. You are gifted at supporting people due to the reality you're an empath. They benefit from your help, and you furthermore take in their uplifting vibes. It is a win-win state of affairs! As it might not use up you, attempt to look for activities to assist a person else and provide assist and assist. Take fee and ask a coworker if they'd like to talk with you for fifteen mins approximately anything on their thoughts inside the occasion that they appear especially stressed out, as an instance. Sometimes all you want to do is speak to a person. Or possibly you could provide greater useful assist. On the tea smash, as an example, you may offer to hold all of us's letters to the shipping branch. Even in case you intend to exchange jobs quickly, acts of compassion and company assist you find out a sense of purpose in paintings.

3.2 Romantic Relationship & Love

The trouble is actual whilst it relates to intimate relationships, whether or not or no longer or no longer you are an empath otherwise you apprehend someone who is. As it is going out, the first rate components for coming across and retaining love are not being attuned to one-of-a-kind people's feelings, continuously being cognizant of energy swings, and proper away being emotionally associated.

Even on the same time as empaths have sensitive souls and loving hearts, they will regularly be their very very very own best enemies in interpersonal situations. It's harsh but accurate. Empaths may additionally make for wonderfully type and useful buddies. However, having an empathic personality moreover makes dating greater tough.

Effective communication with the spouse is a skill which you increase over the years. Your relationship's electricity impacts how nicely you communicate. It hence determines its lifetime. Never in advance than have relationships been so unstable. Divorce & separation disputes are truely so commonplace that they may be not information. It is common to appearance more youthful couples who've previously prolonged past through a divorce. What exactly are we doing incorrectly? Many elderly couples round right here have been companions for years; it changed into common back then. Our connections want intentional strive on our element. A healthy society is the cease end result of sturdy relationships. We have to decorate.

Difficulties in Romantic Relations

The crucial problems in romantic relationships empaths often come upon are listed proper proper right here, together with advice on how to conquer them and feature a more gratifying, balanced love lifestyles. If you're blissfully unmarried and not attempting to find a partner or dates, do not forget the ones sensible guidelines for handling any intimate connection, together with a near friendship:

An Aversion to Closeness and Proximity

Because they fear approximately being overpowered thru using a accomplice's power and feelings, some empaths can also pull away from romance or sexual engagement. Many empaths select a massive amount of physical, emotional, and energy vicinity. It is how empaths withdraw, heal, or provide their overstimulated hyper-perceptive machine a break from absorbing terrific humans's power and emotions. Cheers in case you're an unmarried empath who enjoys it! Do not permit your sensitivity prevent you from relationship or being in a excessive courting if you are an empath. You may moreover have a satisfying partnership and nevertheless want your non-public place. If you are already concerned in a critical courting, giving your self a few me time may probable make it better.

Empath insider advice: Your accomplice doesn't need to be a few other empath to recognize your need for separation. Tell a partner which you want to take normal breaks and give your self room, especially at the same time as your sensitive machine is burdened and overloaded. It can entail spending one weekend participating in social sports, exciting, resting, and regaining mindset the subsequent weekend. If you are already a partner, tell your companion which you sometimes need to take solitary walks within the park, have a examine collectively in bed, or have interaction in some other low-stimulation hobby, on my own or with them. It will deliver your sensitive device time to get better and heal.

Prioritizing a Partner's Needs and Wishes Unconsciously

It took many empath buddies and clients too lengthy to understand they had been putting their accomplice's goals above their own. Empaths can also have hassle putting in themselves in a love dating when you recollect that they are able to experience the energy and feelings of others so carefully. An empath may additionally additionally need to cover their problem rather than raising it with a associate over a widespread acquisition, for instance, to spare themselves the tough emotions their accomplice might experience in the event that they did so. It's how empaths are liable to human beings-appealing in any romantic connection.

Empath insider recommendation: Get better at putting in place your self inside the relationship through manner of the usage of continuously expressing your dreams and dreams. Over time, something turns into simpler with exercise. By turning into more of a spectator and lots a whole lot much less of a feeler subsequently of those conversations, empaths becoming human beings-pleasers may additionally boom stronger pores and pores and pores and skin eventually of arguments. It will assist in keeping in mind that putting your goals and goals first blessings you and your companion. You would probable encourage your companion's self-bad dispositions thru failing to sign your trouble even as you agree with they are developing a awful choice. You deprive your companion of reaping from your creativity and defraud yourself in severa methods if you withhold considered taken into consideration one of your terrific mind that they will reject or disagree with. Recall that partnerships are about compromise; no individual want to be in fee.

Losing Emotional Boundaries

It's critical to avoid merging with a partner in case you're a touchy empath because of the reality people can connect to companions and fans in extreme procedures. If you sense a difficult emotion—which consist of grief or anger—ask yourself, "Is it mine or anyone else's?" due to the truth empaths are perceptive and quite actually select up on what's taking area round them. You can be unhealthily taking on a number of the companion's emotions. When you invest an excessive amount of of yourself in some other's an emotional experience, even superb satisfaction might end up laborious. Consider which you aren't continuously required to revel in the equal feelings as your partner and to allow them to go through their emotional adventure. With companions, you share a stunning, emotional and electricity bubble, however you moreover may also moreover possess a bubble this is absolutely yours. Being privy to that is effective.

Empath's Pro Tips: Develop interests, pastimes, pals, and extracurricular sports incredible from the ones you've got interaction together collectively along with your accomplice. Have grounding sports that help you live grounded inner your energy, including writing, meditation, oracle card readings, solitary exercise, or innovative pursuit. Have empathy-first-rate emotional processing techniques so that you can recognize your emotional barriers.

Attention to Partner with out Comprehending and Observation

An empath's herbal wiring is to apply their clairsentient or touchy psychic channel to faucet into the power of others round them, whether or not it is a group of people, a physical area, or a lover. Being capable of revel in electricity in a room or organization of humans is useful, but if it's far the simplest way you get thru life, it is able to swiftly depart an empath feeling exhausted or overburdened. The nutritious, healthful, and useful desire every now and then consists of tuning proper right into a partner. Sometimes the state of affairs is reversed, in particular if the empath already feels exhausted and overburdened.

Empath's Pro Tips: Discover watching so you can step decrease back and feature a look at your spouse from a extra emotionally and energetically independent angle. You use the claircognizant or intellectual psychic channel whilst you notice and check, so that you preserve to get intuitive records. Being capable of extra intentionally tweaking into or out from a mate while socializing as an empath is a fantastic abilties I assume all empaths need to gather greater approximately.

Regulate Partner's Emotions

Empaths may also moreover moreover mistakenly accept as true with they manipulate a associate's emotions due to the fact they could enjoy them of their our our our bodies. Remember that your associate's emotions are their count. It's usually your enterprise if your lover's feelings crush you or make you uncomfortable. But looking for to govern your accomplice's emotions—as an instance, via constantly looking to calm them down whilst they may be unhappy or speaking them out of a hard emotion—isn't always the pleasant course of movement for every of you.

Empath Pro Advice: Discussing how feelings have interaction may additionally additionally promote emotional maturity and intelligence inside the relationship. Inform your spouse and urge them to get treatment if the way they cope with or show their emotions may be very hard. If your accomplice has anger control problems or constantly studies excessive ranges of emotion that motive them to initiate you, bear in thoughts attending individual or couple counseling classes. See whether or not or not there may be a fashion of being responsible for the accomplice's emotions or seeking to control them by using way of accomplishing a loving self-stock. These self-negative behaviors can also additionally appreciably and favorably change with information and the right tools.

Some Advice for a Happy Romantic Relationship

Empaths location a immoderate price on intimate relationships. An empath also can additionally find it tough to govern the compromises vital to maintain a fulfilling courting. As an empath, you need to make adjustments to have an superb connection. Empaths can use the following advice to installation and hold dedicated, healthful relationships.

Engage in Self-Care

Being empathic makes you extra touchy to distinct human beings's feelings. Additionally, you're more vulnerable to taking over first-rate people's feelings, especially your partner's. You'll need to take care of yourself to save you getting overburdened with the useful resource of it. Make positive you often devour healthy food, exercising every day, and get adequate relaxation. Spend time challenge sports that come up with a sense of pampering and care. Enjoy time doing the sports you need to do, inclusive of analyzing, having a tub, and paying attention to tune. Try consciousness and meditation in case you start to enjoy overpowered with the aid of the vibes your accomplice is sending you. You may moreover find out it much less complicated to differentiate among your sentiments and the terrible feelings you are collecting out of your companion as you become greater aware of your very own goals.

Take Some Alone Time

You'll probable want a few by myself time in case you're an empath. You may moreover resultseasily overstimulate yourself due to the fact you are very perceptive on your surroundings and special human beings. As a cease end result, you'll be required to break up your sentiments from super people's emotions. You might also do this by way of the use of spending time on my own in a peaceful setting. You can also lighten up and quiet your busy essential aggravating device by way of manner of manner of spending time on my own. You might also furthermore recharge your batteries and get prepared for social interaction whilst you spend time by myself. Inform your partner about your want for a few by myself time and why. Your time together may be extra considerable if you do this.

Know Yourself

You ought to find out it tough to differentiate your non-public needs and wants from your spouse's in case you are an empath. Spend some time analyzing about your self to your by myself time. Spend some time identifying what topics to you and for whom. To decide whether or not or not or not changes are required, tune in collectively along with your sensations. Learn what you need and choice out of your courting so you might also moreover set effective limits. A critical first step in satisfying your needs in a courting is knowing what they will be. You can also additionally furthermore have a connection that is extra massive in this way.

Define Explicit Boundaries

You want to create clear limits in case you need to keep your relationship sturdy. You set limitations to defend your emotional and physical well-being. A border need to be expressly focused for it to paintings. You need to provide an reason for why it is vital and what might take area if it isn't always obeyed. A boundary is wanted; for example, if your spouse calls you slurs at the identical time as you dispute, it bothers you. If they call you a slur, you could warn them that this upsets you, and in the occasion that they do it all over again, you'll permit them to recognize and go away. People-pleasers may be empaths. You might probable need to endure a remarkable deal as a end result. But if your limits are doubtful, you may discover your self in an unjust or poisonous relationship.

Be Inquisitive

The moods of their partner are greater perceptible to empaths. It's easy to pick up on the smallest shift for your accomplice's actions, expressions, or frame language. You can also want to assume you knew why the partner modified as you phrase a difference in them. Even in case you are accurate, presuming you're aware of every detail of your accomplice's scenario prevents them from being allowed to specific it from their issue of view. You may also find out more approximately your mate if, in preference to making assumptions, you turn out to be worried. By doing so, you might be able to communicate better and turn out to be nearer.

Consult with Partner

Talk in your accomplice for some time. As an empath, you is probably in a feature to deduce masses regarding others through their frame language. While spoken interplay collectively along with your partner is vital, nonverbal conversation is fundamental. You might also want to have an terrific ear with the resource of way of nature. It may be critical to talk genuinely and openly alongside aspect your accomplice. You'll feel more linked to the accomplice, and your dating will enhance if you percent your thoughts, views, and mind.

Develop Your Capacity For Accepting Criticism

Being criticized may be quite tough for an empath. Any idea of complaint can come out as an attack, and you can cope with it very for my part. Relationship critique might be mainly difficult for you due to the fact you're an empath. It's essential so you can particular your worries in a courting so that you can resolve them. Your spouse have to avoid mentioning essential issues if they will be involved that you may see their moves as an assault. Even despite the fact that having those conversations may not be clean, doing so will maintain your relationship wholesome and sturdy by the use of manner of allowing you to understand what goals every of you have got.

Take Time to be Together

For empaths, in reality widespread interactions are essential. Making small conversations and coping with connections which can be remarkable superficial is probably hard for you. But with out putting any attempt into it, you can anticipate that your sentiments and those of your spouse will live sturdy, mainly because of the truth you treasure your on my own time. A suitable relationship want to include time spent collectively and leisure of shared sports activities activities. By doing it, you and your accomplice also can be part of more deeply and thru shared critiques. It may want to possibly enhance your connection as a associate and draw you nearer collectively.

Express Your Worries

Being an empath makes it easy with the intention to encounter one-of-a-type people's feelings. It might be hard to once in a while distinguish among your sentiments and people of others. It may be hard to clear out thru the various ugly feelings you come across, every from yourself & from one-of-a-kind humans. You probably have an remarkable revel in of at the same time as a situation feels atypical or dangerous. It can also end cease end result from a remarkable deal of worry, stress, or even sadness. Trying to keep the entirety inside may additionally want to make you revel in even greater confused. Instead, you could solve those issues more rapid if you communicate on your partner about your anxieties. You'll experience higher and grow to be toward your partner if you communicate your anxieties.

Relationships take paintings to keep. It can be clean to provide on your relationships in case you are an empath. But it is also crucial that your requirements are glad. The recommendation stated above may be used that will help you in growing a glad and healthful reference to your accomplice. Couples counseling is probably useful if you discover it difficult to preserve a satisfying dating. When you figure at it, your partnership may also moreover furthermore prosper.

3.Three Being in Relation as a Parent

One of the toughest alternatives a person ever has to make is turning into a decide, but empaths find it extraordinarily hard. The widespread upward push in sensory stimuli and bustle overwhelms our sensitive neurological structures.

Despite that, each my empathic clients and buddies who are parents regularly u . S . That they sense the benefits of motherhood a whole lot exceed the demanding situations. They often say that their children are the mild in their lives. Undoubtedly, all mother and father get keep of substantial benefits from raising youngsters. Children can also offer marvel, sensitivity, and pleasure in addition to fostering emotional closeness and a revel in of circle of relatives. Empathic mother and father and caregivers take fantastic pleasure and care in their jobs. Parents can deliver a new child man or girls a respectable begin in lifestyles. Empaths are inherently generous and like playing this feature. They make a holy contribution to their children's improvement by way of the use of the usage of offering their daughters and sons course. Children also are specially effective instructors who offer their parents the chance to growth virtues like love, tolerance, and the capability to set up limitations.

Due to their empathy, intuition, and capability to help their kid's sensitivities, empaths who workout self-care are extraordinary mother and father. But it's miles a primary but—even on the equal time as you are lucky enough to private a useful associate, partner and children, babysitter, or caregiver, the pressures live continual similarly to the innumerable benefits of parenthood. Since they are prone to sensory overload, empaths need to maintain in mind of those stimuli. Less time spent on my own and similarly social touch are a number of those stressors, in addition to a busy day by day habitual with numerous meal steering, grimy diapers, loss of sleep, the everyday screams and cries of youngsters, and as kids grow to be vintage, the severa sports, sleepovers, cluttered rooms, wearing events, and college sports. In mild of this, it's miles absolutely beneficial to carefully preserve in mind the various benefits and stresses earlier than selecting whether or not to end up a decide. Since they're now not pressured to the parenting characteristic or are conscious that it might be disturbing for their sensitive nature, some empaths pick out no longer to have children. Some people are content material to be committed uncles, aunts, guardians, or teachers, roles that need plenty much less effort and time. Others want to have tremendous one child. These alternatives additionally foster a sense of pleasure and belonging.

Ideas for Compassionate Parents

If you're an empath, all the normal parenting pressures may be extended. How do you keep away from freaking out on the equal time as juggling your system and your own family contributors collectively along with your husband, children, partner and children, and co-people, especially if you're liable to crush your self? Having plans to cope with pressure and overstimulation is the crucial detail to succeeding as an empath discern. These abilities may additionally moreover make or damage a figure's sanity and properly-being. Of route, it's miles crucial for all dad and mom, even though empaths have a decrease limit for strain, fear, and sensory overload. Empaths thrive on fidelity, so growing a repertoire of tried-and-real coping mechanisms can let you deal with parenthood's steady u.S.A. Of americaand downs in desire to feeling off-balanced with the aid of them. It's difficult to categorize sensitivity. Although a discern's empathy improves every kids and mother and father mentally, it's far doubtful how it'll have an effect on the determine's bodily fitness. According to a new check published in Health Psychology, empathic parents who often address their children's depression and tantrums be bothered with the useful resource of weakened immune systems and espresso-grade systemic irritation. It is understandable why many medical experts advise strain control practices like exercise & meditation to decorate a discern's immune device.

The following strategies may be utilized by empathic parents and grandparents who are clearly compassionate to reduce strain and keep calm and stability. They will allow parents to revel in strongly while additionally assisting parents in being aware about how they bring approximately their emotions to their kids. When empaths paintings too tough with out rest, they suddenly come to be exhausted. They might be sensible to use those strategies as dad and mom and deliver themselves little moments of breathing room at a few degree in the day. When it consists of reviving energy and tranquility, a touch is going an extended way.

Affirm Gratitude in the Morning

Instead of frantically starting the day with severa to-do lists, this establishes a happy and provoking tone. Begin your day silently or loudly, citing, "I am thankful for on the triumphing time, my well-being, my dating to Spirit, and my youngsters and family. We are thankful for all of those favors. Please allow me to hold my composure. May I stay glad? I desire to be loving.

Breathe

Rushing makes us preserve our breath or breathe , which makes the body annoying. Train your self to take at the least one intentional deep breath to help you lighten up all through your irritating day. You might probably need to use your phone's timer to remind you.

Make Time for solitude

Empaths want to installation as a minimum a few moments of on my own time each day to recharge to cope with the rigors of getting youngsters. If you could, take some time in an area of worship at home or in nature. A five-minute destroy can be all you require if the closet or relaxation room is your sole secure area. Your companion may also additionally watch the youngsters if they may be available. If your youngster is drowsing, visiting, or perhaps at sports sports exercise, you could enjoy a few on my own time. Suppose it is secure to fasten the door on your room and close your eyes to sluggish down whilst your college-elderly youngsters are left by myself.

Play Some Calming Music

Music can lessen pressure and inspire creativity. It can immediately alternate its power. When you cradle your little one to sleep, it soothes you both, and in some time, it may offer peace to your complete household. Even the sound of your preferred track may additionally calm an overworked nervous machine. Of path, listening to track is recovery at the same time as you are on my own your self.

Practice Meditation

Finding quick meditation moments helps calm the worried gadget and halt the cycle of tension. One mother, who is an empath, informed me, "I'm calmer when I meditate. I may not get sucked into my son's tantrum drama, then. Try it out while a cherished one or nanny can watch your kids on the identical time as you meditate for three minutes at domestic.

If you need to meditate brief, do it in the car after dropping the youngsters off or, if no distinct quiet regions are available, in a public lavatory. You may additionally moreover need to invest in a small pond or different water feature for your home in order that the calming sound of water strolling can fill the gap and soothe you and your youngsters.

You can cognizance your interest inside the course of meditation on a relaxing scene like the ocean, the middle of the night celeb, or a forest. You may also moreover try that specialize in how an awful lot you need your youngsters and the manner lucky you are to have them on your lifestyles. It will improve your coronary heart's energy at the same time as you're under stress. Gently exhale constructed-up anxiety as you breathe, center, sense your heart, and re-set up contact with your self & your higher energy. It's high-quality how recovery even a short meditation can be.

Take Short Naps

When your small youngsters are snoozing, you is probably tempted to complete a few laundry, but it's far the precise opportunity to experience a energy nap. You may additionally additionally recharge and get an strength enhance in most effective twenty minutes, in case you need to help you get through the rest of your annoying day. Empaths are greater receptive to receiving restoration electricity even as they'll be sound asleep. Laundry can be dispose of until later.

Establish Limits

Please take some time to set up limits and uphold them. It may be difficult for kids to set barriers, however rejecting excessive requests and unacceptable behavior is good. I've discovered that severa of my empath customers battle with setting limits. They are overprotective mother and father that regularly supply in to their kids' unreasonable demands. Empaths every now and then find it hard to undergo their kids sobbing because the feelings lessen right through them. But having the capability to say, "I apprehend you would love to speak collectively with your pals thru social media, and you may handiest go surfing while you end your schoolwork," is a sign of a superb determine. Or possibly the situation is as follows: "I recognize you want that frosted donut, however it is no longer proper for you. We'll need to give up the shop right away if you do no longer save you sobbing. Then get organized to move away and ditch your buying basket.

Children require limits to socialize. Nobody ever achieves their each preference. They will become traumatic and immodest in the occasion that they do not learn how to manipulate their contamination. The house is considerably calmer while mother and father set honest and tremendous limits and uphold them, selling a extra soothing setting for empaths. Everyone is aware about their barriers and expectancies. Without limits, there may be anarchy.

Avoid Helicopter Parenting

Empath mother and father have heightened instinct and often have a keen experience of what their children are experiencing and thinking. They may additionally moreover due to this have immoderate tension and for that reason stalk and command. But doing it can additionally make youngsters concerned and irritated, which isn't always in their splendid pastimes. Utilize your instincts, however take care no longer to weigh down your youngsters with troubles all of the time. Your anxiety diploma will decrease as you permit float more.

Also, whilst your children are distressed, avoid getting into their private region. Although it is probably tough to look at your children experience grief without interfering, it's miles vital to permit them the possibility to paintings through their feelings. Allow your children to outline their feelings on the equal time as you make a decision which emotions are your responsibility to personal. By doing it, you may additionally permit children to solve problems on their very personal and take in their teachings. While you will although be to be had to help them, it'll save you you from suffocating them or intervening too speedy to clear up their difficulties.

Focus Energies Inward

Knowing the way you show your feelings is calming to your youngsters because it affects their energy. When you are furious, performing out of rage makes them irritated and perplexed. A single empathic mom informed me that her kids had been usually enrolled in after-university sports activities because of her excessive time table. Every time she had a terrible day at paintings, she located that the youngsters ought to act up and complain as speedy as she delivered them domestic. She little by little realized that the idea in their irritability became the electricity. They have been taking in and responding to her anxiety. Therefore, she made it a point to location art work aside as soon as she left the administrative center and as an alternative installation an amusing nighttime with the children. Her kids favorably acquired the change. Her kind and completely satisfied spirit soothed them.

Exercise to Unwind

Stress is launched and comfortable with the useful resource of motion. It lowers pressure hormones and releases endorphins, the frame's natural analgesics. You can relieve anxiety and sensory overload via yoga, stretching, on foot, or hiking. If your accomplice is willing, keep in mind switching up your exercise evenings so you can get in a few hobby.

Enjoy Time with Children

Instead of focusing at the little topics that computer virus you, take into account how cute beings of slight your youngsters are. Concentrate on the honor of being their determine. Children's giggling is healing. By sharing of their happiness, you could help your empath self-lighten up.

Be kind to your self inside the direction of the particular enjoy of raising kids. Recognize your limits and be given them. Even with out children, excessive human touch overstimulates empaths. Even though you will likely need to mention "positive" to a few social invitations, there are times while declining sports activities that aren't vital to you is greater self-retaining.

Chapter 9: Protection And Development Of Empathic Abilities

Being an empath may additionally moreover make you revel in as even though you are doomed in a few manner. The fact is that empathy is a blessing, and also you personal the functionality to use it for your advantage, no longer like any other electricity. The thriller to self-care is recognizing the primary indicators of overstimulation or even as you start to deal with different humans's stress or negativity. The quicker you can take steps to lighten up and cognizance yourself, ever more regular and on top of things, you can enjoy. Here are some hints and hints to extend and defend your empathic competencies.

4.1 Empathetic Traits

The phrases that come from someone's mouth are a whole lot less clean to empaths than the energy round them. One of the reasons you have to no longer deceive an empath is because they may hit upon it. Empaths can also be privy to each other speak in a language they do now not understand, yet they will fully draw close what they are trying to mention based totally totally on their electricity. Empaths interpret electromagnetic vibrations, be aware of one's frame language, and be aware of phrases. Since negativity drains their electricity, they'll be specifically liable to it. On the opportunity hand, a pleasing strength location reasons empaths to loosen up and allow their charisma to spread outward as their sentiments and feelings go with the go with the flow unrestrictedly. Positive electricity recharges and reenergizes

you need a battery.

Due to this, empaths will positioned the entirety of their strength to avoid war of words, get protecting even because it arises, and keep away from specific humans and environments. The frame enters self-safety mode to hold power, so that you do not get fatigued and worn-out. Whether you realize it or now not, empaths can select what and who affects their electricity; they control wherein and to whom it's far directed. Because of the way extraordinary our thoughts are, they're proper away picked up through every body who can music into your frequency. In different phrases, empaths are able to studying people's minds. An adept empath is aware about a way to guard oneself via being gift and clearly privy to everything spherical them just so no person may furthermore penetrate their energy field without their consent. It's important to apply energy properly when you understand how it skills.

Remember that everything you supply out into the area will go once more to you because of the truth what's sent spherical comes round. Energy is much like a drug in that it is much less tough to develop hooked the more you play with it and apprehend the manner it makes you experience. If left unprotected, your energy will go away you, grow to be erratic, and bind itself to three unique electricity transferring via the environment. When empaths are conscious and conscious can without delay discover minute modifications of their environment with out the usage of any of the five senses: odor, flavor, sight, or listening to. As soon as energy is unleashed, it moves forth and in no way expires. Other electricity absorbs it or makes a reference to it because it hangs spherical inside the air & adheres to human beings or topics. You can experience the environment of an area the instant you enter there because our energies solid a mark wherever we skip. The surroundings there relies upon at the attendees or the event taking area.

The superpowers that each empath possesses are listed proper right here, alongside side the manner to use each of them.

Wisdom-Filled Vision

Once conscious, empaths may be able to find out the hassle. We can interpret the underlying significance of sports in our our bodies, organizations, and the wider international. Thanks to this aerial attitude, we're in a position to pull returned from the state of affairs's specifics and address the critical element troubles. When we take ownership of our gadgets and fight for our destiny, we stock once more the lots-wanted peace within the global. Unfortunately, we sometimes feel uncovered due to our potential to peer the coolest in humans. But this extraordinary gift can be a treasured and unusual device even as used carefully. Consider developing your sympathetic abilities in case you're having problems being taken benefit of.

Excellent Instinct

Although every body possesses instinct, empaths' intestine instincts are greater concrete. The solar plexus chakra keeps our enjoy of self esteem and self-admire (Manipura). It holds our revel in of survival instinct, which guards closer to bodily injury and indicators us to high-quality human beings's and awful strength moves. We violate this power at the same time as we override our impulses. Accepting intuitive route requires a strong feel of self and apprehend for that self. Equally critical to restoring and retaining a healthy frame is self-esteem. Our relationships are uncertain, our intuition is faulty, and we enjoy like we have no manipulate over our lives due to our low vanity and regard for ourselves. It takes self-mastery to be a kickass empath and consider and apprehend oneself.

Psychic Power

In addition to having heightened emotional abilities, empaths are psychically tuned. These movements, like instinct, can take many one in every of a kind paperwork. The distinction is that we can now understand someone's situation no matter being masses of kilometers away. Everyone want to be capable of rely on their instincts and solution those who seem to be "calling to them."

The Influence of Your Presence

In the quiet of your presence, you can experience your non-public undying and formless reality because the manifested life strain that sustains your physical shape. Every special individual and animal is deeply infused with the identical energy. You can look through formal and interpersonal obstacles. When you apprehend which you are all one, it is like that. It is what love is crafted from. Because we're empaths, we've got terrific interpersonal capabilities. But how regularly can we make use of this capability to the fullest? We could pick out to shield ourselves in preference to reveal ourselves. We hold our strength to ourselves due to the reality we do not choice to be overpowered by using others. It might be higher to research new skills rather than relying on "the protect." It can be useful if you had self perception to your abilities and will articulate your needs and feelings. Because we're able to experience, see, and recognize exceptional people greater deeply, our presence is a recovery tonic for hearts in need. If we preserve subjects from the overall public eye, we won't change some thing. Because we empaths boom suitable energy, use your natural talents to assist others who're in want.

Power to Heal

On a few level, you recognize you've got were given were given the power to heal both your self and others, but have you ever ever in fact come to phrases with this, or are you still on the lookout for to healthy in? Have you ever felt out of manipulate, despairing, and helpless? Have you ever expert low vanity, lengthy intervals of confusion and disappointment, university dropout, or life-threatening contamination? Did you employ your imaginative and prescient to find out the contamination's root reason? Did you prevent

160

tolerating self-sabotage and use your keen instinct to beautify your self esteem and self-self belief? Did you hire your psychic gift to prevent trying to wholesome in and start accepting the part of your self that makes you specific? Did you discover the manner to use your assertive presence to like yourself surely and take transport of others for who they will be? Have you given up trying to maintain manage over the whole thing? Have you altered your frame and cured your coronary heart together together with your magical skills? Did you regulate the path of your lifestyles collectively along with your revolutionary knowledge? You also can need years and masses of immoderate-diploma resource to trade right into a brave and outspoken man or woman with greater readability and self-assurance.

Creativity

The large majority of empaths are artists. You most in all likelihood perform a industrial business enterprise, exercise recovery, or are hired in a progressive subject like format, paintings, advertising and marketing, movie, shape, or coaching. One of our innate competencies is the ideal potential to translate mind into movement. We are able to bringing our wants to existence. We are visionaries who can benefit mankind through using our abilities. In personal, we're preventing anxiety, disappointment, and exhaustion. Our "government" controls and holds us captive on a country wide scale. We're all seeking to mend the injuries in our souls with meals, booze, capsules, social media, television, and technology. When we awaken, it has vanished. When we emerge from hiding and take possession of our competencies, the sector will transition from worry to like.

We personal particular capabilities. We make our sorrow worse via way of the use of trying to healthful proper right into a hurting environment. With those offers, navigating this international is difficult, but we are capable to perform so through the use of the usage of our one-of-a-type abilities and talents. To understand our full ability, we ought to address the smooth problems that intervene with our each day lives. It alludes to the "wounds" that impede improvement. These scars cause insufficient obstacles and self-unfavourable behavior, which makes us enjoy guilty and irritated. We moreover "maintain it in," whether or not or now not it's far our feelings or the suffering we witness others experiencing. There isn't truthful enough, assertive wording used. We find out it hard to precise our critiques.

The following is a listing of the strategies you must learn how to use your empathic talents. Set difficult, wholesome limitations to hold your composure, equilibrium, and sanity. Establish a effective and powerful energy processing device to prevent unexpected shutdowns.

Tips to Employ Empathic competencies in Relations

Learning to optimistically and in reality kingdom your necessities to experience supported and understood. Stop looking for to in form in and begin being who you're.

Here are a few physical games you could do to apply your superpowers:

If you're an empath, right here are some methods you may harness your superpower of empathy.

Relationship

Show your associate greater affection in case you don't forget they may be hurting or indignant about some detail. Tell them you may be there in the event that they require a sympathetic ear. Your ability to observe your companion's emotions will prevent an emotional breakdown.

Put your self in their position to understand why your associate is disappointed, irritated, or feeling the way they are in the route of a problem or dispute. How could possibly you respond if you professional the identical situation? Being extra empathetic and plenty much less crucial collectively together with your comments in the course of debates might also help you be extra information, essential to a better war.

Increase your degree of take delivery of as real with together along with your accomplice to enhance your courting. Building a more potent courting at the side of your accomplice can be facilitated through your functionality to pay interest nicely and be nonjudgmental. Listen with the aim of records, no longer to get the chance to talk up and make contributions your cents.

Professional Life

When making vital choices at paintings, consisting of selecting your subsequent predominant profession circulate or resolving conflicts with bypass-useful businesses and coworkers, pay near heed to your gut feelings and instinct.

You may additionally moreover assemble closer, more potent relationships together at the side of your personnel via being an awesome listener. When coworkers voice their issues, should you pay attention to what they are saying? Afterward, located yourself in their footwear to actually understand why people enjoy the way they do. Listening to and expertise each other can be a bonding revel in for you and your coworker.

Do you have the impact that a few component is off at artwork? Allow yourself to revel in the feeling and address the trouble earlier than it gets out of hand, or decide out what you can do to avoid it.

Community

Empathy also can assist you recognize the feelings and struggles of others who're masses lots much less lucky than you. Your thoughts-set might also additionally furthermore exchange, as a quit quit result, making you more thankful to your scenario and aware of the fact that no longer every person is as lucky as you. Turn your feelings into some thing constructive. When we are quite charged emotionally, we also can make main changes.

four.2 Methods for Increasing Empathic Super Energy

Empaths fall into lots of kinds. And due to the fact emotion is a feel, it's miles predicted that you could go through diverse levels inside the course of your life. The considerable majority of empaths exhibit first rate dispositions in this situation. Acceptability, an constructive view of existence, a preference to good buy, and admire for communal harmony are a few. As a forestall cease end result, most empaths are specifically reliable and enjoy strongly about their relationships. They are liable to time vampires thinking about the fact that they'll be commonplace aides and fixers. It makes feel that many empaths want to hide their actual selves. The capability to escape, now not rock the boat, healthy in and offer assistance are all examples of this self-protection sort of empathy. Since they reason you to enjoy stressful, wiped out, or worn-out, you will probable every now and then pick out not to attend gatherings, shopping centers, gala's, or unique loud, crowded venues. You also can moreover stay some distance from places you're more vulnerable to experience down or gloomy, like battlegrounds. Like most empaths, you commonly enjoy exhausted and depleted but your satisfactory attempts to attend to your self due to the fact you can't understand various scientific troubles. You do now not must threat your health since you're an empath, this is fantastic. You can use your inherent talents and goodwill in some situations. No, you aren't required to perform above and above. Everything you do to improve yourself in my opinion moreover contributes to enhancing the planet. The highest degree of human boom results from their arrival on our globe. If you're an empath, you may anticipate that you are cursed. The truth is that empathy is a gift, and you have the electricity to harness it internal of your

168

self to emerge as a force in evaluation to each specific.

Being an empath is hard. The truth is that on occasion you enjoy as though you're dwelling in a fable due to the reality no man or woman gets your information and because of the truth all and sundry is normally eating your power. As you are well knowledgeable, the hassle is which you can't return the prevailing to the store to get keep of cash returned; it is yours to keep for all time. You can't forget about approximately your empathic nature. It differs from a creating a tune abilties or an athletic understanding in which you can not simply decide to save you making a track or playing basketball. Being an empath calls as a way to apprehend a manner to guide a fulfilling and useful lifestyles. So, that will help you in doing this, proper proper here are a few novel coping mechanisms.

Taking Responsibility for Your Empathy

Being an empath technique that your undertaking is to like. You were tough to solid the mild on this planet because inception. The first step in growing the inner moderate display is identifying why you got here right right here.

Use your Gut Feeling

As an empath, you're very aware of distinct people & your surroundings. Learn to agree with in yourself if you could check others' minds, apprehend intuitive imagery, stumble on scents, or revel in some thing on your gut. You can also keep away from power snares and establish trusting, deeper relationships through the use of the signs you get.

Never Portray a Victim

Sometimes the guilt starts offevolved to devalue itself. After some time, the yearning to be precious turns into a victim mentality. It generally happens in religious relationships at the same time as the mentor gets all the cash, and the enthusiasts lose their revel in of nicely really worth, their supply of earnings, and plenty of others.

Define Limits

Set ultimate dates in your interactions with power vampires after you become aware about their use of your energy. Keep in thoughts your behavior and memory at the same time as you're with them. You'll in the long run be capable of leave and reclaim your treasured strength really. You'll have loads extra unfastened time to have interaction in sports activities you enjoy.

Empaths want time to rejuvenate, so that they meditate. Meditation is a brief and powerful method for growing empathy. A three-minute cardiac meditation, as an example, will assist you experience focused and robust within the middle. It is right for improving your stamina at the same time as you begin to revel in sensory overload. No, lying down isn't essential for meditation. Instead, spend time in nature or attempt to see your self as being in a defensive cocoon that is impervious to evil energies simply so mild might also moreover skip thru. Act frequently a day.

Using Breathing

Make it a ordinary to sit down down and deliberately breathe whilst you meditate. As you breathe in, take into account importance and possibility. As you exhale, recall breathing out any bad electricity. Even higher, say, "I possess the potential to respire. I exhale my stress and fear." Use this method regularly each day to launch the body's saved stress.

Getting Rid of Bad Vibes

As empaths, we usually supply some of horrible strength with us. Utilize techniques for reworking horrible power. Bring plant life in your administrative center to useful resource with strength absorption. Additionally, search for crystals that would modify the supply of herbal sources. They seduce you to the middle. It could assist when you have been positive whilst confronted with a hard scenario. When appropriate, seeing the humor in a scenario might also furthermore remodel toxic emotions. You also can begin each day with the aid of thanking it for its functionality to promote correct vibes.

Esteeming Oneself

The purpose of life is to attend to your empathic self. Only with the aid of searching after yourself first are you able to do all you need to. Self-empathy is listening to one's emotions and thoughts. Be fantastic to renowned your sensitivity and recognize your feelings every day. Be conscious that you will be sturdy and delicate on the equal 2d. Enjoy on every occasion you research some element new or take movement to beautify your nicely-being. Remember which you additionally alternate lives while you stay up for your capability. You will enjoy superb satisfaction whilst you certainly consist of your empathetic element. At a deeper level, you'll realise the fascinating simple photograph.

Additionally, you may get get proper of access to to extra strength through manner of repute in line with Origin. Once you recognize the fundamentals of empathy, you may experience a fantastic transformation on your lifestyles. So, be cushty and understand your lifestyles.

Value your Creativity

People which can be empaths have a tendency to be alternatively modern. They revel in dancing, painting, and drawing considering that those sports are all particularly soothing. You want to preserve the globe from its many troubles, and despite the fact that that may be a noble goal, the fact is that it's far impractical. By the usage of your imagination to explicit yourself, you can do away with horrible electricity and bring some trouble adorable that you could alter and be lucky with. It moreover serves as a manner of releasing some resentment related to failing to treatment the area. Find a skills you have got and art work on it every day.

You will experience a tremendous deal much less and disappointed about being an empath in case you encompass artistry on your everyday sports activities.

Make your House Heaven

You need to experience solid in your very own vicinity and make it a place in which you enjoy definitely comfortable. Your home's environment and mood need to correspond to the manner you revel in it. You will want to make a few changes if your residing state of affairs is unsatisfactory. How might probably you describe your fabric cloth wardrobe? Your shelves? What's beneath your snoozing bag? Are topics stacked and crammed everywhere? As you have were given examine, energy actions and clings to physical topics, living matters, and exclusive energy. You begin to experience wiped out, dejected, worn-out, and disenchanted whilst you are round many unpleasant individuals. You have a experience of serenity, health, and power control at the same time as you're in a putting with effective individuals. Let's examine how having a clean and messy residence would in all likelihood have an effect in your temper.

The disadvantage of Messy Home

The repercussions of an unclean residence are indexed under.

Makes you Feel Worn Out

A messy house is like an energy-sapping vampire. Being round something with horrible electricity connected will put on you out.

Sows a Sense of Hopelessness

An infinite mountain of mess is mentally exhausting. Even cleansing seems vain since you take into account you may in no way cease the whole thing.

Advantages of Clean Home

It promotes serenity. In a smooth house, you could unwind and relaxation. There is room to move spherical, and you recognize in which the whole thing is. As soon as you input a inn room, you feel cushty due to how neat and nicely-stored the distance is.

Enables you to Feel Good

Messes constructing up dust and mould. Are you usually sniffling and wheezing? Have you ever skilled hypersensitive reactions? You are most probable breathing in all the dirt in your own home, this is the motive. Cleaning up your own home for spring will help your health problems.

Gives a Sense of Control

How might now not it sense as a way to locate subjects without troubles? Positive power can't go along with the go with the flow through a cluttered environment. Remember that electricity connects itself to matters, and sickness draws horrible electricity, which results in fatigue, paralysis, and annoyance. How does it experience to have trapped horrible power to your body? You need to live in mattress and block out the arena because of the fact the whole thing is getting more hard, and you have not any concept why.

Unblock Energy through Decluttering of Home

Here are some effects while you enjoy the clean domestic.

Increase Vitality

You'll enjoy more vibrant and attentive after you carry order and harmony into your property. Clutter removal eliminates imbalances and obstructions out of your private area, like acupuncture gets rid of them from the frame to boom properly-being and dynamism. The maximum attractive components of your persona come to life while you walk thru regions that have been ignited with new strength due to the truth you're inspired.

Avoid Negative Thoughts

Each terrible addiction has a purpose. Do you select out out to study TV whilst mendacity on your mattress as opposed to sitting on the

178

sofa because of the truth you are too lazy to fold the laundry accumulated over the previous six months? Or probably it is due to the reality the mattress symbolizes sleep, and if you climb into mattress after paintings and try to do the ones important devices to your to-do listing, you may fall asleep. When you have cleaned the couch, you may take a seat down on it while you get domestic from art work to study your preferred TV display, however while it's over, arise and preserve the challenge.

Problem-Solving Skill Increases

Your residence will experience extra open and spacious as quick because it's been cleared out, making it much less hard to pay hobby and imparting you with a trendy outlook on your problems.

Get Rest

Regardless of ways masses sleep you acquire, are you continuously exhausted? Bad electricity is trapped a number of the clutters you have pushed below your mattress. Once your room is prepared, you may word that high nice vibes can flow into with out problem all through the distance, making it much less hard which will get an amazing night time time's sleep.

Mess delaying you could come up with greater time. You constantly lose gadgets if your home is messy. You waste time searching out items like a sandal, a hat, or a pockets because of the fact you can't get them, which reasons you to be late for activities like artwork or social activities. You may want to probably preserve greater or an awful lot much less an hour an afternoon via decluttering your house because you might not must undergo piles of gadgets to find topics.

Improves Sense of Intuition

A clean environment produces a enjoy of guarantee and readability. Peace of mind comes from know-how wherein the whole lot is. You also can deal with staying inside the gift second at the same time as your thoughts is at ease. You will discover that it's miles plenty less difficult to make massive judgments even as you want to. Giving your private home an extensive cleansing must take some time, but you can no longer remorse it once you're finished.

Regular Yoga

Yoga is an powerful way to help release surplus power. To release tension and blocked strength, quite a few postures, respiratory deeply, and meditation are important. You need to permit your existence strength to float freely within the route of your body to free up your self from putting onto suffering, whether or not or now not you're non-public or someone else's. So, that will help you get going. Also to be had are books, DVDs, and yoga training.

Breathing Techniques

Put your hands to your knees even as sitting at the ground at the side of your legs crossed and also you're again right now. Keep your eyes closed and inhale thru the nostril; your stomach will upward thrust. For 4 seconds, keep your breath. Four seconds of exhaling must purpose the stomach to increase. For five mins, maintain doing this.

Yoga Poses to Release Bad Emotions

To assist you in casting off awful electricity and allowing correct power to go along with the drift resultseasily all through your frame, right right here are some yoga positions.

Dog Facing Upwards

The key to casting off bad emotions is inexperienced communique. This yoga pose aids in beginning and balancing the throat chakra and easing throat pressure.

Place a mat at the ground. Legs extended inside the decrease again of you, ft driven into the floor even as you lay to your stomach. Put your fingers right behind your shoulders, flat at the mat. Breathe in and raise your higher body off the floor with the assist of your fingers. Exhale at the same time as you are repute upright. Continually inhale and exhale on the identical time for 10 seconds.

Bound Angle Pose

Our hips keep a substantial amount of our emotions and feelings, and trauma. Your hips will become more bendy way to the attitude-certain stance, which helps the frame's trapped electricity go together with the float. On your mat, sit down down together collectively together with your legs crossed, but let the bottoms of your toes contact. Spread your arms over the ft as although you have got were given been starting up a e-book. Inhale deeply, then extend your backbone higher. As you exhale, loosen your knees and allow them to drop to the ground. Ten times, repeat this.

Plank Position

The plank feature is beneficial for the CNS and for strengthening your center. Your functionality to handle any troubles that might come for your manner will growth even as you enjoy bodily and emotionally strong. The arms want to be genuinely beneath your shoulders at the equal time as lying to your belly. With your shoulders apart and your feet firmly planted on the floor, stretch the legs in the back of you. Take a deep breath and lift your fingers and toes off the floor. Hold this posture for 10 seconds at the same time as breathing in and out simultaneously.